MYSTERY
OF JOY

◆ ◆ ◆

By Chris Padgett

Authored by Chris Padgett

Cover design by David Calavitta
Interior design by Casey Olson

Copy editing by Colleen Stepanek

Published by Life Teen, Inc. 2222 S. Dobson Rd. Suite 601 Mesa, AZ 85202
LifeTeen.com

SPECIAL THANKS

◆ ◆ ◆

To Linda - You have seen the entirety of who I am and continue to love me nonetheless. You are my greatest picture of God's unconditional love. I hope to bring you joy and spoil you for the rest of our days together.

To Life Teen for the opportunity to collaborate with them in ministry.

Finally, to my family, who allow me to experience a bit of heaven in our joyful, sorrowful, glorious and luminous moments. What an amazing life we have had thus far!

TABLE OF CONTENTS

• • •

INTRODUCTION

◆ ◆ ◆

◆ ◆ ◆

I wish we could sit down and get coffee together. I love people and enjoy sharing my faith, and if you picked up this book you are the kind of person I would drink coffee with. The chances are good, however, that we may never meet for that cup of coffee. So, this book is the next best thing.

If we did sit down for coffee, you would start to learn a few things about me. You would realize that even though I am an introvert I love making people relax and find humor in our humanity. You would know that I am not afraid to talk about the wounded and broken parts of my life. We would talk about what has made me upset, frustrated, sad and what has left me broken and the ways I've been healed. You would also recognize that I've found joy in all of these moments because I know God's love for me is steadfast. He is not waiting for me to get my act together before he loves me. I have been loved, am loved, and will be loved by a God who is not afraid of my mess. This brings me great joy, and you may ask an honest question, "How can confidence in God's love bring you so much joy, even when life is a total mess?" The answer to that is a mystery which I cannot totally solve, but I can come close.

Many people in our world want to set up following Jesus and being happy as two things that are opposed to each other. Is it possible to be happy and faithful at the same time, or does following Jesus doom us to a life of becoming a sad saint? Can we even find joy and meaning in our times of sorrow? In John's Gospel, Jesus says He came to bring abundant life (John 10:10). I think we all want to live an abundant Christian life, but we are not sure how that exactly works. What does it look like for us to truly be filled with God's love? Though this kind of joy may seem like a mystery, I can approach it by using some other "mysteries." The mysteries I am going to use to help us understand what it means to live an abundant Christian life come from the mysteries of the rosary.

I realize that right now you might now know or even care about the rosary (yet). Consider this, though: When we pray the rosary and contemplate the mysteries of the rosary, we look at the life of Jesus through the eyes of Mary — the person that knew him best — and that is powerful. Saint John Paul II called the rosary a "compendium of the Gospel." I encourage you to start praying the rosary as you read this book. Right now, you just need to know the four sets of mysteries within the rosary. These are groups of meditations based on the life of Christ, as witnessed through the eyes of Mary. Each set is made up of five individual mysteries. The mysteries of the rosary — joyful, sorrowful, glorious, and luminous — are primary categories that apply to everyone's life and current circumstances.

Whether you pray the rosary daily or have never picked up a set of rosary beads before in your life, this book is structured to help you dive in wherever you are most comfortable and you should know a couple of things about how I wrote it. This is not a "typical" Marian book that looks at the sweetness of Mary in an attempt to try and mold us into something we are not or seemingly unable to become. I am a firm believer that Mary wants us to be ourselves in loving her Son, Jesus. This is not a deep theological reflection on only the mysteries of the rosary. You don't even have to know what the rosary is or have ever prayed it to enjoy this book. This book is about a simple truth: The abundant Christian life is found in our joyful moments, but also our sorrowful, luminous, and glorious times as well. These are parts of our shared human experience. Since the mysteries apply to all aspects of our lives, I will use personal stories and invite you to ask some serious questions about where you are on your spiritual journey.

The first section of this book is a short reflection that challenges us to ask what we really believe about life, death, and knowing Jesus. Anytime we sit down to pray a rosary we begin with the Apostles' Creed — a reminder of the basic tenants of our faith. The next four sections of this book are based on the joyful, sorrowful, glorious, and luminous mysteries. In each section, there are five reflections that focus more deeply on the specific mysteries within each set.

Section Two: The Joyful Mysteries. This section examines the joyful moments of our life and how Christ is present within them.

Section Three: The Sorrowful Mysteries. This section calls us to reflect on sorrowful moments of our life and how Christ walks with us in them.

Section Four: The Glorious Mysteries. This section invites us to look at the glorious moments of our life and how Jesus rejoices with us in them.

Section Five: The Luminous Mysteries. This section reflects upon the luminous (or enlightened) moments of our life and how Jesus speaks to us within them.

The final section is another stand-alone reflection that challenges each of us to continue to live our faith well, recognizing that a joyful life is the best preparation for eternity.

In each section, we will see the mystery of a joyful humanity, in good and bad times, which we are all invited to experience and that experience begins and ends with love. Jesus wants you to fall in love with Him because He loved you first. When you allow yourself to be loved in the joyful and sorrowful moments of your life, those that are glorious and even insightful and illuminating, I believe you will find a world that is filled with meaning. I hope you find a lot of joy in this book, even if you are invited to look at some of the difficult moments in your own life along the way. So, until we can one day get coffee in person, pour yourself a cup (or two) and let's dive into the Mystery of Joy.

SECTION ONE:
THE CREED

◆ ◆ ◆

◆ ◆ ◆

The Game of Tag
and the Ambulance

◆ ◆ ◆

I believe in the
resurrection of the dead.

"You didn't finish the game."

The small figure of the neighbor boy came in and out of my view as I struggled to catch my breath. For some reason, he kept staring at me as the squealing of a dozen seven year olds echoed throughout my house during a game of tag. I did my best to respond without frightening all of the kids. "Mr. Padgett's tired." I gasped. What I wanted to say was, "Mr. Padgett is dying."

My wife had already called the ambulance, and I wondered if this was what it was like to die. I was stupid, really. What business does a man over 30 have playing tag with kids a fifth his age? For whatever reason, I declared that, "Mr. Padgett will play tag," and told them they all had until the count of 100 to attempt to hide from my keen all-seeing eye. As soon as I hit my 100 count, I shouted, "Ready or not, here I come."

I summoned speed beyond my physical ability and rocketed up the wooden stairs and tagged small screaming kids all along the way. I sped through the upstairs hallway, continued down the tiny stairway leading to the kitchen, through the dining room and finally into the entryway of our home when I realized I was not really breathing. My heart beat irrationally and my sense of panic grew. Every labored heartbeat reminded me that I should not have given chase to such athletic children. I fell into a fetal position on the floor and tried to find a cool space for my body, simply hoping to breathe.

I looked up at the terrified face of the boy above me, and became upset that I ruined my daughter's special birthday party. She would need to explain to her friends that her father was whisked away in an ambulance amidst the waves of sirens, making our home once again the talk of the town. My thoughts were interrupted as I felt a cold sweat break out all over my skin. I started breathing again, and I knew that I could recover if I had time to rest. The ambulance arrived, and the medics checked my vitals, asking me if I wanted to go to the hospital with them for further evaluation. I thought, "Hey, you all are the experts here, not me!" I decided to stay at home and take it easy, since they are professionals and didn't insist that I go. I was scared, but also too young to be concerned. A month later I was told that unless I had open heart surgery I could die within six months. If you were wondering, I haven't died yet — I haven't played tag since my daughter's birthday, either.

There is one thing that is true for all people and that has always been true: one day we are going to die, leave time and enter eternity, and somehow what we do here in the "now" will impact and determine our destination "later."

I have a difficult time pretending life isn't worth celebrating or worthy of being cherished because I have been aware from a young age that life was fleeting. With all the negativity that exists in the world of social media, news programs, and internet websites, my hope is to lift your spirit to see God is bigger than the mess of your past, the severity of your sin, the finality of your illness, or the constant anxiety of past regrets. God is bigger than the obstacles you face, fears you clutch, and the worry you cannot name. He wants us to have abundant life and I have found that abundant living is best expressed within Catholicism, which not only knows how to redeem suffering in Christ but also guides us to find joy in all circumstances. I have found that within my journey toward Catholicism, I was given hope and purpose in a way that I previously didn't realize I lacked. After over 16 years of being Catholic, I still face my mortality with joy. Somehow, my weakness gives me strength in Christ, and the reality that I will one day die inspires me to live a life that impacts eternity. These paradoxes don't make sense outside of the Christian context and that is OK. Most of us don't have constant moments of sorrow or joy; in fact, most days are a little bit of both. Where is Christ in all these moments that seem to ebb and flow around circumstances and fleeting emotions? He is with us. We need to ask ourselves if we really believe that because if we can't start with that basic reality, then the rest of what we talk about regarding joy, suffering, glory, and finding light in darkness won't make a lot of sense because then Jesus is just some historical figure (at best) or a work of fiction (at worst). We need a person that experienced what we experience and someone that walks with us today.

In Jesus' life He experienced moments of great joy, sorrow, glory, and times when He brought light into darkness. When we reflect on the life of Jesus through the rosary, we can start to find places where our story and His story line up. Right now you may find yourself in a season of sorrow, glory, or enlightenment. Regardless of where you are now, we are going to start our reflection with joy and the places we most clearly may find "life in abundance" (John 10:10).

Reflect:
Right now in your life do you consider yourself in a time of joy, sorrow, glory, or a place where you are learning and growing deeper in your faith?

SECTION TWO:
THE JOYFUL MYSTERIES

◆ ◆ ◆

Annunciation to Mary

Visitation to Elizabeth

Nativity of Our Lord

Presentation of Jesus

Finding of Jesus in the Temple

As we reflect on the Joyful Mysteries, I want you to think about the joyful moments that surround the story of your life. Where have you experienced joy? In the following reflections you may wonder why some stories have elements of struggle and even sorrow. Think about your experiences of joy; sometimes our most joyful moments were preceded by concern, panic, or even sadness. We work hard and spend long nights studying for a test, but feel joy when we get a good grade. We push hard and hustle for a promotion and in the moment it is hard, but then we get the raise and new job. We have our heart broken and feel great sorrow, but then we meet someone incredible who helps us find healing and we fall in love in a new way. Those can be moments of struggle and pain, but they lead to joy. Finding contentment in difficulties is an amazing grace, but we can all admit that it is a wonderful feeling to find yourself getting what you longed for even if it took an extended period of time. I think St. Paul gives us insight into this type of lifestyle when he says he has learned to be content in times of plenty and in times of want (Philippians 4:12). When Christ is in your life, there isn't a lot to worry about.

◆　◆　◆

My Favorite Part

◆ ◆ ◆

Annunciation to Mary

When my son Joseph received his first Communion he looked adorable. Our family had just moved north of Syracuse and we asked our new parish priest if he would accommodate my crazy travel schedule and offer my son his first Eucharist on a Sunday I would be home. Little Joseph had finished first Communion preparation, but my schedule prevented him from receiving the Eucharist with the rest of his class. With the move and our life literally in boxes, it took a little longer than we would have liked for him to have his first Communion. Our priest was gracious and not only did little Joe have his first Communion, but we were able to have extended family attend.

The following week I sat next to Joseph during Sunday Mass and after the Liturgy of the Word, as we prepared for the Liturgy of the Eucharist, Joseph leaned over and whispered to me, "This is my favorite part." I looked at my son and asked him why. He said, "Because this is when I get to receive Jesus." I barely kept it together. He waited so long to be able to join the rest of his family and fellow parishioners that, for him, there was nothing obligatory about being at Mass. Joseph looked with anticipation to the moment when he received Jesus in the Eucharist.

I know most of us have sat in Mass waiting impatiently for the Eucharist because we realize it means Mass is almost over. I've been a Catholic for 19 years, and even though I am still in awe and wonder that I am given the chance to receive Jesus in the Eucharist, I still have felt distracted and antsy in Church. I often travel on weekends, and after I do my presentations at ministry events my body goes into complete meltdown mode. As an introvert, being around people is draining and sometimes after a long event I can barely function. Usually events I do end with a Mass, and it takes everything I have not to fall into a deep sleep during the liturgy. At one particular event, I settled into the back of the parish (as all Catholics are prone to do) and settled in for the liturgy. I was exhausted and tried my best to present a prayerful posture as I leaned my head against my hand. Just as the lector finished reading something from the Old Testament I heard a snore. To my embarrassment, I realized it came from me. I sat up, stretched and popped my back and tried to refocus. I leaned forward, elbows on my knees and hands on my cheeks. I was terribly close to the lady with triplets in front of me when, before I could help myself, another snore made its way out of my nose. The woman in front of me didn't even flinch. Most of Mass I repeated the same cycle of falling asleep, waking up, and trying again.

When I finally got to Joseph's favorite part and humbly walked up to receive Jesus, He was so kind to me. Jesus' love for me was entire and present even when I was more like the disciples falling asleep in the garden (Matthew 26:40). His love for me was not minimized or restricted because I was exhausted.

I am not sure what your day has been like today, but I do know that Jesus awaits to give Himself to you in the Eucharist. We don't have to wait for Sunday to be blessed by Him, as you well know. Think of the Annunciation, where the Spirit of God came upon Mary. If you have a Bible close by, open it up and read through Mary's encounter now in Luke 1:26-38. Each Mass we have the chance to receive Jesus and go out to change the world. That is truly worthy of our thanksgiving. Even when we struggle and are distracted at church, Jesus gives Himself to each of us nonetheless. I wonder if we meditated upon the Eucharistic gift more often if we wouldn't have more of a child's heart and echo my son Joseph saying, "This is my favorite part." You know what I think? It is likely this is Jesus' favorite part too, because it is when He gets the chance to love us in the most intimate way on this side of eternity, even if we might be a little drowsy.

Reflect:
Where do you encounter Jesus in your daily life? Where does He come to meet you? What effort do you make to go meet Him?

◆ ◆ ◆

Happy / Sad

◆ ◆ ◆

Visitation to Elizabeth

It is funny to me how similar my kids are to the mannerisms, quirks, and idiosyncrasies of my wife and me. Even though they are like us in some ways, they are still so unique. Each child handles conflict, stress, and moments of joy so differently. While they are in fact our offspring, they are so singular in how they approach life. As a father, I am amazed at the way each of them has touched my life in different ways and made me a better man.

Many years ago I was doing ministry in the diocese of Des Moines, Iowa. I was starting a friendship with someone who would become one of the most important people in my family's life named Bob Perron. He was the Diocesan Youth Director and ran a camp all summer long in Panora, Iowa. It was while I was at this camp that I saw Bob implement this idea of highs and lows, or, as I eventually called it, "happy/sads." After an action packed day, filled with one activity after another, Bob would take the leaders of the camp up to the chapel and ask them what the "high" of the day was. Every person had a chance to share the best part of their day, followed by the "low," or worst part of their day. As I sat listening to each person willingly disclose some of the more difficult moments of their day as well as allow others to join them in their joy-filled moments of that day, I realized that this was something I wanted to do in my family.

Within the Padgett day, there is no guarantee that all the children will be together at the same time at any moment. There are sports and play practices, concerts, and church events. If you are like us, there are sleepovers and homework assignments that seem to go on for countless hours. In other words, we are busy. To implement an activity that would include all of the family was difficult, but we realized that dinnertime was our best bet to try this new activity. I told my kids that I wanted them to tell me about their happy part of the day and their sad part of the day. Each one took to it quite easily, and the next thing we knew we had a little family tradition. It was always funny to me how the smallest kids were the most eager to tell us what their happy/sads were. Their hands would fly into the air, begging to be the first to start the evening sharing, and when you called on them, you could see that they didn't have anything prepared to say. So we'd wait, and laugh, and roll our eyes, listening to spur of the moment happys and spontaneous, and often times silly, sads. It was a way for us as parents to, in a subtle way, teach the kids the importance of sharing what their life was like.

In our family, we realized that there are often seasons we experience; some seasons we find ourselves clicking on all cylinders, while other times it is apparent that we are out of sync with life and each other. We get busy and often forget the importance of sharing our happy and our sad moments with one another. What I've learned, though, is that when we actively and intentionally care about one another's day, giving them the opportunity to habitually disclose their moments with the family, we teach them not only to take note about where they are at in their journey but also about the importance of community.

I believe that we need to get into the habit of disclosing our happy and sad moments to others, especially those within our family. I am confident that this is a practice needed within our spiritual family, as well. Think about how at every Mass we acknowledge to one another that we have "greatly sinned." Why do we disclose this sad part of our humanity to one another? Because our sinfulness and brokenness are universal. Do you know what else is universal? God's love, which is greater than the sinful and broken parts of our life. Our "sads," the things that we have done and the things that we have failed to do, are all given the opportunity in each Mass to be united with the universal love of God. In this willing offering of self-disclosure, we can be a part of a miracle. Our sad becomes a happy. Many of us have heard the phrase "Oh, happy fault," as reference to the sin of Adam and Eve. The goodness of our God, the joy in which He comes to us, is of such magnitude that we are redeemed and centered back into our true humanity. Our sad is transformed in the joy of the Gospel.

Joy comes from sharing the highs and lows of our lives with each other.

Mary, the mother of Jesus, had a cousin named Elizabeth. She and Zechariah, her husband, weren't able to have children and were old. I am sure that both of them felt pretty broken. They may even have felt like God gave up on them. Through their lives, there were a lot of sad moments. Zechariah is surprised when God gives him some big news. If you have a Bible close, read about it in Luke 1:18-20. God wasn't done with Zechariah and Elizabeth, yet. Think of the joy they must have felt after waiting for so long — they went from a place of sadness to a place of joy. That kind of joy needs to be shared — Mary goes to celebrate with her cousin.

Think about Mary visiting Elizabeth. For Elizabeth, the conception of her baby is a major "happy" moment. She has waited to be a mom for decades, and now her dream is being fulfilled. Mary was also joyful, but perhaps in a different way. Mary may have wondered how people would understand her unexpected pregnancy. She, as a young woman, trusted in God but not without a degree of human anxiety mingled with her joy. Both women rejoice when they see each other — they share the highs and lows of life, the happy and the sad moments, as family. We call the moment the two meet "The Visitation." It is a moment so joyful that even the baby that Elizabeth is carrying feels that joy (and the presence of Christ in the womb of Mary).

When you go to sleep at night and think of each of those moments that brought you joy, remember that God can take the sad filled parts of your journey and turn them into opportunities — even allow them to become avenues — of joy. One way we do that is by sharing those moments with others to help us celebrate when life is good and to carry us when life is a struggle.

Reflect:
What is your happy and sad moment from today? Who could you share this with? (As an extra challenge, go share it with them within the next day.)

◆ ◆ ◆

Blobfish

◆ ◆ ◆

Nativity of Our Lord

For the last few years I have been using slides during my keynote presentations. The pictures I select are intentionally hilarious and funny in and of themselves, but I find that I have an uncanny ability to enhance the humor with my commentary. I feel that if it is funny to me, it will likely be funny to someone else. Recently, I used a picture of a blobfish when I was talking about my "beach body." I set up the slide with me talking about being in "great shape" and the need to be humble and grow in humility; I told the audience to keep all that in mind while I shared a picture of me swimming. This was the cue for my blobfish picture. The blobfish is an ugly fish to begin with, and the picture I used was especially nasty because it looked like there was a green booger seeping out of its mouth. What is amazing about the blobfish isn't that it is simply so ugly (which it is), but that this fish is also poisonous. Many animals have protective qualities to keep predators at bay. Poison is an extreme deterrent, but I wonder why that is necessary for the blobfish? It is so ugly, and nothing about it would seem to be appealing in terms of a meal, so God making this fish poisonous seems excessive. But I trust God had a plan for this unique fish.

Have you ever wondered what was going through our God's mind as He crafted the animals? Clearly it is impossible to know, but I have a feeling He smiled and laughed as creativity became flesh and blood. His thoughts took on breath, and His desires came into existence. God intentionally created the blobfish to look the way it does, with the added bonus of being able to poison those crazy enough to try and attack it. There was no limitation to His creativity, and in the end, it was good.

I don't think it is a reach to imagine that God was smiling as He crafted and predestined you. You may have aspects of your appearance or personality that you struggle with, but I do believe God had and continues to have great joy as He looks at the uniqueness of your life. It can be hard to see ourselves the way God sees us. In many ways, we are conditioned to fall in stride with the world's view of beauty and influence because the world is noisy and demanding. Letting God's view of you dictate what you think and how you live is certainly ideal but often very difficult to apply. Ultimately, God didn't make any accidents, and while we can laugh at the oddities of some of God's stranger creations, the special place humanity has within the created order is nothing to be cynical about. God created the human person to stand above the created order, to be special and unique. There is nothing accidental about you because God is not second guessing His creation, to which you belong. It is easy to poke fun at ourselves and wonder if we should be taller, smaller, thinner, fatter, freckled, or fair. But if we were to step back and take a breath, we would realize that God joyfully considered and willed our existence so we may as well joyfully live this existence with a tenacious and gregarious heart.

God doesn't leave us alone, though. God steps into our creation through the mystery of Jesus' birth. The second person of the Trinity, God the Son, takes on human flesh so that we can be saved. Think about a manger scene, maybe you have one at your home. That scene is profound and not because the animals are all well behaved in their adoration of Jesus. It is profound because God values you (yes, specifically you) so much and sees your creation as having so much potential and worth, that God takes on the reality of our creation and lives among us as one of us. He comes humbly in a way we wouldn't expect — as a baby. We may wonder why an all-powerful God would choose such a humble and unassuming way to enter into our existence, but through it God speaks something powerful. He is like us in all things but sin. He experiences our created existence like we do. He feels what we feel. He is with us.

Reflect:
How do you view yourself? Do you see yourself as created good, worthy, and deserving of love? What does the Nativity of Jesus tell us about who we are?

◆ ◆ ◆

Dream Home

◆ ◆ ◆

Presentation of Jesus

What is it about buying a home that can be both so exhausting and rewarding? In our family, we have chosen to be people who dream a lot. We don't simply live our life with pie in the sky expectations; rather, we dream big, and then we work hard to make those dreams come true. No one will ever be as motivated to succeed and bring about your most adventurous dreams than you. My wife and I decided to be very intentional about our dreaming, and this most recently displayed in our move to New York state. One of many funny things about the Padgett family is that we are not impressed or interested in buying the biggest mansion we can find. In all honesty, my wife has an assessment about our society's modern lifestyle that I think is spot on. She says that it is interesting how we, as a society, spend most of our money on a home that is so big that it usually keeps us within rather than encouraging us to explore the outdoors. Of course, she is obsessed with being outside since it is her "happy place," but I believe her assessment is right. We didn't want a huge house in New York. We wanted land and the freedom to make a life and sustain ourselves from the work of our own hands. We wanted enough space to build barns for animals and hay, create trails to go cross country skiing, and have the option to walk outdoors and go hunting on our own property. When we talked about our dream home, it was more than just a building. We didn't want a mansion so we could stay inside; we wanted a lifestyle to bring our dreams to fruition.

Over a year ago when we really started exploring homes, our options were next to nothing where we were living. When the door opened for me to begin to look in other states, Linda and I spent time traveling and looking for an area that we could call our own. We took a walk on what would one day be our property and the odd nine-sided home seemed so insanely fitting for a family as unique and adventurous as our own. The deer tracks and hundreds of maple trees not only promised game for hunting season, but syrup in the cold months. Everywhere we looked, there was potential.

After a long process, we finally closed on our home in central New York. I was so excited and hope-filled. Linda mentioned that for us to move into this new dream home, we would need some massive miracles to take place. The year process of moving toward the fulfillment of our dream was so difficult, leaving us aching at times, and there were moments when we felt like we were going to be forced to give up on a dream that we both were certain God had placed within our hearts. After we signed the contract, I remember looking at Linda and telling her, "Congratulations, we are now officially broke."

Moving in was exhausting as we had to go back and forth to Ohio so many times to bring up numerous loads. We took our time unpacking and cleaning but almost immediately began the analysis of what we had and what we would need to bring this unkempt land into good homesteading order. Light switches seemed to be connected to random parts of the house, and circuits were unmarked and seemingly fickle in their reliability. We found the weirdest old farm equipment scattered about the property and an old disgusting deep freezer that looked like it was once in a horror film. The water was from a well and had a unique color. The kitchen, which had the laundry room in it, was placed in the hottest part of our home, so whenever Linda cooked or did laundry it was as if we were transported back into a tropical nightmare.

With every problem we found a way to get things into a basic semblance of order. Water was tested, the electric issues addressed, and the septic was emptied. It seemed every other day there was some major expense that had to be addressed for our basic survival. Our dream home was still everything we knew it would be eventually, but it was going to take some time. We needed a refrigerator, our washing machine gave up the ghost, and vehicles had check engine lights on and had to be fixed and inspected before we could even get the New York tags. Everything cost more and more money, and then on top of it all we needed to pay our end of year taxes. Regardless, even with all of our obstacles, we both knew that we were exactly where we were supposed to be. This was our dream, and we were going to tackle whatever problems we faced.

What I began to realize is that the ultimate dream is never without its obstacles and problems. Part of what makes a dream so spectacular is the journey toward its being obtained. Realizing this was a very freeing moment for me, because I was under the delusion that once we got our dream home all would be smooth sailing. To grasp and hold onto a dream means that a lot of work was done to bring you to that moment, but the maintaining of that dream necessitates a continued effort and energy many do not nurture.

When you think of the dreams that are on your heart, I hope that you pursue them with a tenacity that is unmatched. I hope you are not swayed from your effort and distracted from your goal. The reward of holding or being in the dream that you've longed for is in and of itself a rush; to maintain and grow in that dream will realistically mean you must work even harder. Is that worth it to you?

Now, ask yourself, "Is it worth enough for you to let God have?" We work hard for our dreams and that tenacity can turn into a desire to withhold our dreams and desires from God. We don't want to ask for God's will to be done because we are worried He might take the dream and smash it. As part of Mary and Joseph's religious practice as a faithful Jewish couple, they were required to offer their firstborn back to God through a ritual at the temple. The purpose was to recognize that the good things we have — especially the blessing of a firstborn child — are gifts from God. A couple would bring their firstborn son to the temple and the priest would offer the child to God. Then, the couple would "ransom" the child back from God by making a substitute offering (two turtledoves or a lamb). It was a reminder that we are stewards of the gifts that God gives us, including our dreams and desires. God places those things there for a purpose and to hold them and nurture them is a blessing. For Mary and Joseph, it was a profound moment because the child Jesus was God's Son, yet God entrusted them with this incredible gift. God has entrusted you with the dreams you have. We have a responsibility to invite God into those dreams, ask for the grace to complete them, give God permission to change them (if they will be bad for us), and then we have the duty to work hard to honor them.

As I write this, I am heading back home to my homestead after traveling. I am thankful for the chance to walk onto my property and be home. The odd-shaped house, the messy property, and vast amounts of projects needing to be completed make me feel happy because they are gifts from God. I am learning more about how to work and maintain a dream, and I know that we are leaving a legacy for our children that shows them that you are never too old to start anew. That is how we have lived our life, and it is how we will continue to live in our older years. Why? Because we have a responsibility to honor God with the gifts He has given us — and there is great joy in living that kind of life.

Reflect:
What are some of the gifts God has given you in your life?

Room Service

◆ ◆ ◆

Finding of Jesus
in the Temple

I recently finished doing an event in Michigan that was held at a very nice hotel. I was free the first evening I arrived since the event wasn't slated to begin until the next morning. After sound check I told the host I would likely go up to my room and settle in. My host encouraged me to relax and told me to charge any meals I ate to the event. I did this by just writing my room number on the bill and she would take care of the rest. I was pretty excited. An evening to relax with nothing on the schedule was a rarity for me because I usually travel to events on the same day that I am slated to present.

In this hotel there was a fancy restaurant on the top floor that overlooked the river. The view was breathtaking! I sat down and ordered a drink and a soup, just taking it all in. My first thought was that I wished Linda was with me to enjoy the view. She would have loved it! I ordered a steak, and, I must say, it was exceptional. I ended up with a light dessert and found myself very rested and content. When the bill came, all I had to do was put my room number and name on it and the event took care of it. All of the meals were like that. The event organizers even paid for me to be picked up by a professional transport service. I didn't have to worry about paying a tip because the venue that brought me in had already done so. I must say, I even felt a little guilty because I was being treated so generously. I mentioned to my host that I was worried that my dinner was so expensive, and her response was, "It is the least we can do."

What is the least we can do? What is our minimum for loving people? For the event organizer, the "least" was still a very high standard. It reminds me of a passage in Sacred Scripture where Jesus talks about a man that was hurt, battered, and left wounded on the road. All of the religious and elite members of the society walked past this broken man. The "least" they could do was literally nothing. The story changes when a Samaritan man came and brought this hurt individual to a place where he could be healed and get needed rest. The Samaritan offered to pay all expenses, even anything that went beyond the deposit he had put down with them. Charge it to the room! The story shows us that we must remember that all we have is a gift from God, just like we reflected on in the last mystery, but we go a step further. We remember that, since we have been gifted, our minimum for loving others is actually to try to love them like God loves us. We give to others as things have been given to us. That attitude not only impacts those we love, but those who see the way we love others. Think of the innkeeper who received the wounded man. The Samaritan was a witness to generosity that likely astounded the establishment. Samaritans were loathed by the Jews, and here was one helping the other.

How can we be generous to those who are in our life? How can we invite others to "charge it to the room"? Pondering these questions made me think about a girl I met recently; this girl was so happy because she had, previous to our meeting, emailed me and I had actually emailed her back. This may seem small, and in many ways it was, but for this young lady it was above and beyond what she expected. Once when I was at an event in Ohio, the people who had brought me in mentioned a young man that really loved the ministry

I did. We went out of our way to let him know he was special. Even more randomly, I was once stopped at an airport by a young redheaded girl who told me she had decided to come back to the Church after hearing a talk I gave. You would be amazed at how a small act of generosity can speak volumes.

I could probably fill a book with the ways people have amazed me with their generosity, but let me simply draw your attention to this fact: When we are generous with others, we show them what God is like. God, who is generosity, invites us to consider those around us as people worthy of recognition and respect. We hear the word "prodigal" used in reference to the story in Luke's Gospel, and many assume it means "to be selfish" or "to deviate from the straight and narrow." Actually, the word prodigal means "to lavish." The story shows three primary people who lavish themselves and others in different ways. The younger son lavishes himself with selfish behavior. The older son is resentful and filled with pride. The father lavishes his son with forgiveness. The older son spent time in the father's house, but never really knew the father. His minimum level of love was nothing.

The final joyful mystery is the finding of Jesus in the temple. Jesus is only 12 when the narrative takes place and His family is returning form celebrating Passover in Jerusalem. In the midst of the chaos of leaving Jerusalem, they lose track of Jesus. When they realize that they left Him behind, they return to Jerusalem and find Jesus in the temple. When they told Him they were worried, He responded simply, "Didn't you know I would be in my Father's house?" If we want to love like the Father, then we need to spend time with the Father, truly getting to know Him. As we experience the love of God the Father, our hearts change and we start to love like that. The minimum level of love we can offer goes up.

We are called to be like the father in the story of the prodigal son. We are called to be like the Good Samaritan. We are called to be like our Father in heaven and, through our generosity and love, bring other people into the house of our Father.

Reflect:
When is a time that someone gave you more than you deserved? How can this moment help you understand God's generosity and mercy?

SECTION THREE:
THE SORROWFUL MYSTERIES

◆ ◆ ◆

Agony in the Garden

Scourging at the Pillar

Crowning of Thorns

Jesus Carries the Cross

Jesus Dies on the Cross

As we approach the sorrowful portion of this book, I think it is fitting to ask: How can joy fit into such a difficult category? Is it possible to be happy and faithful, even when we experience great sorrow? I believe the only way we can find happiness or, more properly put, joy in difficult times is by understanding the Catholic teaching of redemptive suffering. Each of our difficult moments, whether it is something we experience personally or see happen to someone we love, is an opportunity to unite our pain and agony to the cross of Christ, believing there is a redemptive possibility. In other words, our suffering has value when united to Jesus' suffering. Without the work of Christ, there is nowhere for the pain and agony of our sorrowful moments to find new meaning and ultimately resurrection. We can't expect to live a life of constant joy. Eventually, in heaven, there will be no more tears and pain but, for now, life can be difficult. Is it possible to find joy in our pain? In Christ, I believe we can.

The stories I have chosen to give to you in this section all deal with loss and the reality of death. If we can find the joy of Christ here, we will certainly have something the world desperately longs for: meaning amidst seemingly meaningless moments.

◆　◆　◆

Saying Goodbye

◆ ◆ ◆

Agony in the Garden

Maybe one of the reasons I ritualistically watch "It's A Wonderful Life" every Christmas is that, in addition to it being a classic, it seems to speak about something greater than just holiday celebrations and family gatherings. It goes much deeper than the average movie and wrestles with a primordial question of life's meaning. Does my life here on Earth matter? If so, to whom? We get a tiny glimpse of an answer in this cinematic gem. The main character sees how different the world would be without him. He sees the real legacy he is creating and, ultimately, that is what we all want.

The matriarchal influence from both my paternal and maternal grandmothers greatly impacted and shaped me. These two women were forces of nature and not to be toyed with. From the former, I learned how to laugh and savor joy; from the latter, I was shown how to live with adversity and how to cling to one's faith with an entire devotion.

I was on an airplane a few years ago, traveling to share the faith, when I listened to a voicemail from my mother. She usually starts off every message with "Heellllllooooooooooo, it's your mother…" as if I couldn't tell! Her tone on this call was far more serious and that itself was telling. She wanted me to come and say goodbye to my grandmother, who was well into her 90s and now in hospice care. She told me that my grandmother was still alert and said it would be nice for me to come and say goodbye one last time — to see her and remember — to which I readily agreed.

My maternal grandmother, Arda Perkins, never saw me with her eyes. I know that sounds a bit odd. For most of her life her sight was extremely poor, and she was blind before I arrived on the scene. Her eyes "gave up the ghost" as she flipped a mattress while cleaning, causing her retina to detach. Now you would think this would have caused her to discontinue her efforts of cleaning, but she was manic in her efforts at cleanliness. Apparently, eyes were of little consequence to her when it came to this virtue so aligned to godliness in earlier generations. As a small child, her blindness was something I usually associated with the dog she used, folded dollar bills in her wallet to ensure she gave the grocery lady the right amount, bruises on arms from bumping into walls, and countless hours of reading coupons to her while she decided which to keep and which to discard. She was entirely blind but seemed to see things clearer without her eyes than most do with perfect vision. She probably decided early on to wrestle past the limitations of her handicap as best she could, and, in all honestly, I never heard her complain about being blind — ever. I have so many memories of Arda cooking croissants with little chocolate chips rolled into the flaky bread, fists filled with senior olympic gold medals from walking and swimming competitions, and her grabbing my arm and allowing me to lead her from one area to the next, which was an outstanding responsibility for me because I had eyes with which to guide us. She, in some way, was the moral compass for our family, guiding by example, showing us what trust in God looks like even when hardships and difficulties were present daily. She would sit for hours listening to the Bible read from her small tape recorder, all the while knitting one and purling two. She prayed for me daily and I am confident that is why I travel the world speaking about faith in a God we can't always see so clearly. Sometimes, what we can't see isn't as important as what we truly know.

Linda and I bought tickets, prepared for my daughters and sons care while we were away, and made the trip to southwest Florida. I remember thinking that the room my grandmother was in was quite pleasant. My uncle Ernie was there, having traveled from Utah. Both he and my mother had fiery red hair in their younger years, but it was now primarily gray with hints of a reminder of earlier times of mischief and taller frames and healthier times. The somber countenance of each one present was not enough to keep our smiles at bay, and somehow in the severity of my grandmother's failing health we found joy. How odd, and yet how refreshing.

The days all seem to mix for me when I try and recall specific moments, but during the early encounter with my grandmother, Arda, in that hospice bedroom, I decided to somehow weasel myself into the single bed with her, and she attempted to move over and provide room for one twice her size. Her face was wrinkled but not beyond recognition, with lips sunk into the chasm of her mouth, unable to support themselves with her dentures placed conveniently on the bedside table. I leaned over and whispered in her ear: "I love it when you don't wear your teeth." She burst out laughing. I wish you could have heard it. I must say, her laugh was more like a cackle — a three packs of cigarettes a day type of laugh — yet as far as I knew, she had never smoked in her life. The thing that you can't tell about this moment is that it was terribly personal, and I am not sure my sister, mother, or uncle could realize just how beautiful it really was.

My youth was filled with days of asking her to take her teeth out so that I could see her lips sink into her mouth. For some reason it was an amazing appeal for my comedic personality and something I had no way of doing with all of my teeth firmly set in their proper place. On very rare moments, she would relent and out they came to which I gave lavished and gratuitous thanks, savoring the mystery for the rest of the day.

I am not sure exactly when I asked the question, but it seemed silly to pretend that we had all gathered around her bed to just encourage her to take another bite of tapioca pudding. She was dying, and she knew we were all there because her time had come. I held her frail and liver speckled hand and asked, "Grandma, how can I pray for you?" With her unseeing eyes, she looked toward me and said, "Ask for courage." I have been amazed by the honesty of this answer for years. She was the holiest woman I knew, and she really didn't have a lot of huge sins to keep her from the pearly gates as far as I could see. Think of how many sins we would avoid by simply not seeing! She didn't drink, didn't smoke, and never swore. This is not to imply that she was the Virgin Mary, but I am afraid I have sinned more in a year than she did in 97 years. I assured her I would pray for her to have courage. It was such an honest moment with my frail but strong grandmother and for that I am grateful. In many ways she tried to show me how to live life committed to Christ, and, here at death's door, she was showing me how to die.

It was so wonderful to be with my family, and, at one point, my wife reached out to me and suggested that we let her know that it was okay to go if she was ready.

Arda wasn't eating, and she was so small, wrapped with bed linens, almost swaddled there in white. I leaned in to my grandmother and whispered, "Grandma, you should know that Jesus considers you to be one of His closest friends." And again, with profound honesty she said, "I hope so, because He's one of mine."

As I walked toward the door, having to make my flight home, I knew that I would never see my grandmother again. Reaching for the doorknob, I stopped and turned around and went to my grandmother one last time. I just wanted to say goodbye again, and I am glad I did. She lived an amazing life, filled with love and faith, and she was historically old as far as we were concerned, but even then it is never easy to say goodbye. My mother called a few days later and told me of her mother's passing, and since my final goodbye, I have treasured the time I had to say farewell.

After her passing, I had great hope knowing that she was finally able to see. I remember praying as a child that my grandmother would regain her eyesight. She had countless surgeries but none restored her vision. In my childlike faith, I prayed that God would do what the doctors could not, and I remember hearing the Lord say "no" to me. I was shocked and asked why, to which He responded, "Because I want the first person she sees to be me." It wasn't an audible word He spoke, but that answer spoken to my heart gave me a lot of comfort. After my grandmother's passing I realized that my grandmother's first gaze into the eyes of Jesus was probably unspeakably beautiful. Without earthly vision, she had seen the beauty of Christ, but the beauty she must have seen when her sight was restored in heaven was probably indescribable. My grandmother left that legacy to me to pass on — to share Christ's beauty with others — and by God's grace, I have accepted the challenge. When I think of Arda and her legacy, these lyrics put it best: "...was blind, but now I see."

If I got my way, my grandmother would never have received that beautiful "first look" at Jesus. God's plan is better than our plan, even when we don't fully understand. Jesus was in the Garden of Gesthemene the night before He was crucified. He invites three of the closest disciples with Him, but they can't stay awake. Unlike my family as we gathered alongside my grandmother to wish her goodbye, they don't realize that this is the last time they will see Jesus before He dies. Jesus prays in agony; He knows what is coming and asks God the Father that, if it is His will, that Jesus could pass the cup of crucifixion. But then Jesus prays something profound — He lets go of His will and accepts fully the Father's will. In the face of suffering and death this is a difficult prayer to pray. We should absolutely pray for miracles, like I did for my grandmother, and we should ask with big, childlike faith. But the flipside is we must also accept whatever God desires for us with the obedience of a child, as well. Ultimately, even if the path involves suffering, there is new life.

There are a lot of people who, at an early age, have to say goodbye to loved ones. This vivid preview into our own mortality can bring a variety of responses to each of us. It is likely that some of you have already buried someone you love — perhaps even someone very close to you like a sibling, spouse, parent, or friend. While it would be amazing if we could all have the chance to see our loved ones live long and healthy lives, passing from time into eternity only after we've had a chance to say our goodbyes, that is certainly not the case for many. For those family members and friends whom you mourn today, know that your mourning is proof of a deep and profound love for one who touched and shaped your life. There is nothing wrong with feeling that loss deeply. If you did not have the chance to say "goodbye," our God is not limited by space and time, and I believe He gives you a chance to speak clearly and without hesitancy to those whom you loved. After all, God gave us those loved ones because He knew they had the potential to aid our journey toward Him. Spend a little time thinking about what a gift your loved ones who have passed were, and let it motivate you to savor the people still present on Earth. We are not guaranteed tomorrow, but we certainly can celebrate today.

Reflect:
Where do you struggle to accept God's will and where have you experienced suffering that led to new life?

◆ ◆ ◆

His Overestimation

◆ ◆ ◆

Scourging at the Pillar

"I think I have to use the bathroom." We both looked at each other and the reality of what my friend said was so exciting. He had to pee! This was truly the fruit of a great miracle.

I met Brad soon after moving to Steubenville, Ohio. My wife and I were settling into the every day routines of our family and my pursuit of higher education, and what we noticed about this tiny, dirty town in the Ohio Valley was that it was filled with wonderful families who had a love and passion for the faith. I can't remember how I first met Brad and his family, but somehow I nudged my way into their lives. He was quiet and strong even though his body was weak, and engaging — he had a fire behind his eyes that you just wanted to be around. Brad's family lived just around the corner for a time, and then they made their way to the next town over. They found a little house and some land and were, simply put, a holy family. Brad had kidney disease and his body, at least when I met him, was not treating him kindly. I have memories of finding great joy in bringing a smile to his face, usually through my silly behavior, but I think I was like his television (which he didn't have) and he found entertainment in my company. They found me refreshing (I hope), and I found them fascinating. It was like a modern day Little House on the Prairie family brought to us from the past and placed on our doorstep. When his family visited, Brad would take a small sip of his wife's beer, knowing that even that taste would be something that needed to be addressed at his next dialysis. We would talk about faith, books, illness, and healing, and throughout those brief times together, I found myself struck with so many thoughts. One time, Linda and I were sitting in their home discussing illness with them. I spoke of my heart condition, the surgery that left a scar going down the center of my chest, his numerous kidney transplants, and other wounds from illness and said, "Wouldn't it be amazing if we were both just healed? I mean, we would retain the scars, but what if at our next checkup, your kidneys and my heart are just perfect?! Wouldn't that be an amazing miracle and a great witness to God's healing power?" He agreed, but then said, "But I have to believe that since our Lord suffered, it has to be the better way." Good grief! I knew he was right, but he couldn't even chop wood due to the exhaustion of the disease, and he had difficulty lifting his children. He was very sick for crying out loud, and yet he found Christ in his illness.

On Christmas Eve, a miracle occurred for Brad. Several months prior, Brad was taken off the donor list for a new kidney. His health was so poor that when he received new kidneys the disease attacked them immediately. The result is that the doctors determined he just wasn't a good investment for a new organ. We had a mutual friend who went into the waters at Lourdes on Brad's behalf, and as a result Brad regained enough health to be put back on the donor list. Brad's doctor felt that he had found a prescription cocktail that would allow Brad to keep the kidney this time, so all they needed now was a kidney to arrive. That Christmas morning Brad received a call telling him to hurry to Pittsburgh because they had a kidney and the medicine to make it work this time. Upon receiving the call, Brad ran through the house, yelling to his children that their dad was going to be well. The whole community celebrated, and everyone was elated at the news. After the surgeries and recovery, I was given the amazing opportunity to bring Brad home from the hospital. I was so excited! When I got to his room, he looked smaller and frail but was ready to go home and begin the long journey toward healing. It was a snowy mess out, and I remember thinking, "Please God don't let me kill us on the way home for crying out loud!" He had gone through so much for it to end with a nasty slide into the ditch. And that was when he said it: "I think I need to use the bathroom." We pulled into the McDonalds, and he urinated with childlike joy. For him, it had been a long time since he had the opportunity to do so, and I, with overzealous excitement, suggested we get a lemonade and try to fill the bladder up again.

I dropped him off at his home, and immediately upon his arrival, he ran into the bathroom and threw up. The medicines he was on were so strong that his body just reacted like that. Whenever possible I drove him to the doctors in Pittsburgh, just to spend time with him. One day I remember Brad, looking at me after we got into the car, said, "I gave my body to God a long time ago to use it for His glory. Sometimes I think He overestimates my strength." I said something like, "I'll have to quote you on that one day." Unfortunately, that day came sooner than any of us expected. Brad mentioned to me that he felt there was something not right with the medications; he was struggling more than normal.

My travel schedule picked up, and I was on a trip, working in Florida, while my friend was dying in a hospital room in Pittsburgh. I was riddled with guilt. I wanted to be with him, but it was not realistic. I heard a deacon was there with his wife, praying the rosary in the room that evening. It was the feast of St. Thomas

Aquinas, his favorite saint, and his wife said, "Don't you leave me, Brad, unless the Blessed Mother comes for you." She was nine months pregnant with their seventh child when the Blessed Mother came for Brad. So many people knew him longer and could share the beauty of Brad's life with you with much more detail, but the small time I had with him has continued to bless me for over a decade. I miss making my friend smile.

"I gave my body to God to use for His glory." That line still resonates with me. In the second sorrowful mystery, Jesus is whipped and beaten at a pillar. It is a visceral, terrible reminder that the body of Christ was given for us. The suffering Jesus endured was intense and loved ones could only look on — helpless. It felt much like watching Brad suffer, but for Brad his suffering was united to something bigger. His body was, in a spiritual way, united to Christ's body. Saint Paul tells us that our bodies are temples of the Holy Spirit, they belong to God and we should use our bodies to glorify Him (1 Corinthians 6:9). Many people read this passage and think about the good things we should do with our bodies and the ways we should avoid sin, and that is certainly true. But we can also give glory to God when our bodies start to fall apart, fail us, and even suffer toward death.

When I was a Protestant, certain movements within the charismatic movement emphasized the "health and wellness" Gospel, insisting that we didn't have to be sick and that we could certainly be wealthy if we followed God's plan and had faith. Brad had more faith than any televangelist I saw, because he chose to believe in God's love for him and his family amidst the weight of such a draining disease. There was, in my past, such an inability to deal with mortality, with weaknesses and sickness. Why do bad things happen to good people? Because the human condition is messy, people's choices have consequences, and basic genetics can be unrelentingly unfair. God is with us in our suffering; knowing that, seeing that, and believing His presence matters is enough, even if you are fading from time into eternity.

I don't know what challenge or illness you are facing today, but I want you to remember my friend Brad and his family. There are answers to prayers that come in ways that seem to be the exact opposite of our requests, and while we may never understand why, if we can hope and believe (faith) that this God does love us, we will endure. You can endure! Don't give in to despair; it is possible that God has found you privileged enough to be one of the few whose sufferings play a significant role in emptying purgatory and bringing the faithful here on Earth closer to their final end. Thank you for your gift of suffering. This is something I never could understand in my Protestant past, but now, with the guidance of the Catholic Church, I find the teaching of redemptive suffering to be such a miracle for the majority of the population who haven't found themselves rich or without any sickness.

Reflect:
Is there any area of your life right now where you are experiencing bodily suffering? How can you view this suffering as something that gives glory to God? Do you know someone that is suffering from bodily illness? Write down three prayer resolutions to offer up for that person daily.

◆ ◆ ◆

Call Me by My Own Familiar Name

◆ ◆ ◆

Crowning of Thorns

My father's side of the family has never been very religious, as far as I can tell. When my paternal grandmother passed away a few years ago, those who'd made their way to Detroit for her final days were of the general mindset that while it was a great loss she had lived well into her 90s and had left a wonderful legacy. My father didn't want to inconvenience my sister or I by insisting that we come up and had tried to persuade us not to add one more thing to our already busy schedules. But, eventually, because my uncle had his two children make the trip to Michigan, my father decided that having his children come wouldn't be so problematic after all. I was relieved. My wife and I drove the five and a half hours to my grandparents home, and I was given the opportunity to lead our gathered family in a memorial wake of sorts. I think, since I was the most religious member of the family, they concluded that it would be more appropriate for me to speak instead of employing some pastor from a random church who didn't really know Phyllis. The service was at Oakland Hills Golf and Country Club, which in so many ways was funny, perfect, and clearly put together by my grandfather. I think if he could have had his remains placed under the 19th hole (the bar) he would have. The Club was the nicest place in the area, and my grandparents had spent countless hours and a lot of money there over the years, so it seemed fitting to all in attendance that we remember the matriarch of our family at this specific place. I was nervous, and I had my notes scribbled out on a paper, crammed between the pages of my Bible. I'm pretty sure they are still in the same exact spot. I began like this:

"I know we aren't supposed to have favorites when it comes to our grandparents but my grandmother Phyllis was mine. To be honest, I am quite certain I learned how to laugh and seize the joy out of every moment because of this woman. She was effortless in her ability to laugh, spend my grandfather's money, and make my sister and I feel at ease."

We laughed that afternoon as I told stories about my grandmother, and soon others willingly got up and remembered Phyllis. It was a very unique afternoon, but I ended my reflections with a poem I found. This is what I read:

Togetherness

"Death is nothing at all — I have only slipped away into the next room. Whatever we were to each, that we are still. Call me by my own familiar name. Speak to me in the easy way which you always used. Laugh as we always laughed at the little jokes we enjoyed together. Play, smile, think of me, pray for me. Let my name be the household word that it always was. Let it be spoken without effort. Life means all that it ever meant, it is the same as it ever was; there is absolutely unbroken continuity. Why should I be out of your mind because I am out of your sight? I am but waiting for you, for an interval, somewhere very near just around the corner. All is well. Nothing is past; nothing is lost. One brief moment and all will be as it was before — only better, infinitely happier and for ever — we will all be one together with Christ." (*The Holy Souls: "Viva Padre Pio,"* *1988, pg. 183*) *Carmelite Monastery, Waterford, Ireland*

For me, this poem has been a great comfort, and I have shared it with a number of friends who lost their loved ones. The part that always stands out to me is the portion about calling out to our loved one with such a genuine familiarity, because while they are not seen by us here, they are with us nonetheless. This is a very Catholic idea and a great consolation. "Call me by my own familiar name." Indeed! When we die and enter into the beatific vision, the qualities that were virtuous here on Earth are exponentially increased in the presence of Jesus. So, for example, if we are encouraged to pray for each other and come alongside one another here on Earth during difficulties, how much more will that virtue be enhanced and perfected in the presence of God? We don't take an indifferent attitude toward our family and friends who have yet to finish the race! The interdependence between the Church suffering (those in purgatory), the Church militant (those on Earth), and the Church triumphant (those in heaven) is very important for the Christian to understand. We on Earth can offer our difficulties and struggles as a gift to Jesus, uniting all to His salvific work, resulting in redemptive ramifications for those being perfected in Christ. The intercession of the Church triumphant on our behalf here in time is invaluable, and fostering relationships with those who have gone before us is encouraged. Many saints know what we are going through and can pray for us in a way that is perfected in the light of Christ.

The concern for some is that asking for the saints' intercession, or calling to our loved one "by my own familiar name," could be considered praying to the dead, which is forbidden in the Old Testament. Here is the consolation we can hold to: In Christ, we are more alive once in His presence than we are here on Earth. We are limited in our ability to understand and pray here on Earth but we are encouraged to do so. When we are in God's presence, we can pray with a specific effectivity granted by God in a way beyond our ability here in time. So, for our family members that have passed away, we have the opportunity to pray for them and offer our struggles up to Jesus' salvific work on the cross on their behalf. For those family members who have passed away, we can ask for their intercession and aid as we journey along. We are a body, with Christ as the head, and our interdependence is a grace from God, ensuring our greatest possibility for perfection.

The third sorrowful mystery turns to reflect on Jesus' head, specifically the crown of thorns He wears. The "familiar name" of Jesus is Messiah and king, but the crown of thorns is meant to mock both, but it communicates something more about suffering, redemption, and reveals who Jesus truly is as king and head of the Body of Christ. It is through the suffering of the crown of thorns that we are offered a share in the crown of Christ — in His Kingdom. For some of us, death is the crown of thorns we wear. In Catholic teaching, if we die still attached to earthly things, we enter a state of being called "purgatory" (where the Church suffering are located) in order to detach from anything that might hold us back from heaven. In a way, we are crowned with thorns — there is a feeling of suffering with detachment — but that crown gives way to a heavenly crown. For this reason we should offer prayers for those that pass away, especially for people who we may have struggled with. Just like the prayers of the saints in heaven impact us, our prayers impact those in purgatory.

Pray for your family and friends who have passed away. Offer your sufferings to Jesus on their behalf, and ask for them to intercede for you. It is an amazing chance to collaborate together and continue to grow in love with one another as we all seek the crown that Jesus has waiting for us when we enter His Kingdom.

Reflect:
Who is one person (living or dead) that you feel needs your prayers? Who do you need to ask to pray for you?

◆ ◆ ◆

Prayers and Drawings of a Child

❖ ❖ ❖

Jesus Carries the Cross

When I was a small child, my father and grandmother took me to an "old folks home," or, more acceptably stated, an adult living facility, to visit my great-grandmother Wonderlich. I was relatively young, and as was my custom, I lagged behind while weaving a youthful line of exploration as I ignored the insistent commands of my elders to hurry up. There was an old man in a wheelchair near the entrance who seemed to be sitting peacefully. He motioned for me to come and shake his hand. Some of the memories from that day are faded, but of this I am sure, when I shook his hand, he would not let it go. I remember my heart galloping in my chest as I frantically looked for my family to intervene. They were walking down the hall unaware as I tugged my hand harder and harder in attempts at freeing myself from this deceptively strong senior adult. I somehow got free and ran down the hall, sneakers smacking the marbled floor making enough noise to disrupt the old and dying. The place always made me uncomfortable, and maybe it was that initial terror that was the cause of my discontent, but it may have been the entire environment. Everything seemed like it was held together with antiseptic, strong perfumes, and glass vases with flowers placed on handmaid doilies. There was little to captivate a child. I was just beginning my journey of life, while everything around me in that place was nearing its end.

Many years later my wife and I were living in southwest Florida, which (interestingly) has many senior adult living facilities. One afternoon my wife suggested we have our kids make some Valentine's Day cards and take them to the elderly at the facility near our home.

I was less than interested. In my heart, I knew it was a great idea, and in some ways I wanted to be a part of this work of charity, but I was also busy. Linda asked a few more times, and I eventually relented and decided to join them, all the while keeping my eyes peeled for an old man in a wheelchair with a tenacious vice-like grip. The nurse who walked us about was so kind, and all of the grandmothers and grandfathers were elated at the little drawings and our children's smiles. We finished the first floor and took an elevator to the second floor to finish handing out our cards. Finishing our rounds we approached the center island, thanking the nurses and readying ourselves to go. There was a man in a wheelchair (you knew this was coming!), and I nudged my small daughter Madeline to go and give her last card to the man. I was watching like a hawk as she gently placed the card on his chest. It was odd that he didn't take it from her, or even acknowledge how cute she was, or even say "thank you." After a few moments he began to rock a bit and moan. I almost yelled out, "Get out of the way!" as I moved forward to guard my child, unsure of what might happen next. As I walked closer to him, I could see tears running down his face. His moan was his only way to express his emotions, as he cried and rocked. He had had a stroke and was unable to speak or move. The card upon his chest touched him, and I have never forgotten that moment. I realized how we can find joy in tears, and how even our most seemingly insignificant efforts can be a blessing to others if done with love. My daughter's picture was a typical little kid's drawing with a circle and lines coming out of the ears for arms, more amoeba than art, yet the man knew what the card was; it was a gift.

This wasn't the only time my daughter Madeline helped me learn something. It was an early Sunday morning, and we were making a mad dash to church to try and arrive on time for Mass. Things were crazy, we were running late, and, to save some time and potentially get a seat, I dropped my wife and kids off while Maddie and I went to park the car. As we got out of the car, a man who was homeless confronted my daughter and me. I had seen him before; he loved to come to the Catholic church because he realized most of us have some residual guilt and will likely give him money. But on this particular day, I was in a rush. I told him that I didn't have any cash on me, but if he was hungry after mass, I would take him to get some lunch. He looked irritated at me and began to walk away in a huff. I wanted to yell at him and tell him why he shouldn't be mad at me. I wanted to remind him that if anyone should be angry, it was me. I was selfish as usual. It was at that moment that little Madeline looked up at me and said, "Daddy, I have money." She held her small pink purse in her tiny hands, and I suddenly felt my heart melt. I wanted to tell her that she was not giving her money to this guy, but the Holy Spirit encouraged me to keep my mouth shut. I looked at her and called the man back. I handed him a dollar, asked if he was sure he needed it, and explained that my little girl was willing to give her own money. He took the dollar and walked away. I don't even know if he said thanks. Part of me was very upset at the man, but the majority of me was in awe as I looked at my little girl and recognized how sacred that moment was. She gave such a seemingly insignificant gift, and yet, I think all of heaven cheered that day. I wish I could be more like her.

When Jesus was being led away to be crucified, He was given a cross. We reflect on that journey in the fourth sorrowful mystery and often reflect on the crosses we carry. In a couple of the Gospel narratives, though, there is a second character with Jesus during this moment. Simon of Cyrene helps Jesus carry the cross. He bears the suffering of Christ. How well do we bear the suffering of another person, even when we don't have to? We can journey with people in big moments and in small moments; simple acts of love like a card at a nursing home or a dollar of spare change can be enough to help another bear their cross. Sometimes we help people bear bigger crosses like an illness, job loss, or walking with someone as their family falls apart. In those moments, we take on some of what that person is suffering with and carry it as well. For that reason, it isn't always attractive to help another bear a cross. Why willingly embrace suffering if you don't have to? Because there is joy in that. There is love in that. There is hope in bearing the cross of another because we know that the cross leads to resurrection, and by helping someone carry that cross, we carry them closer to that moment of resurrection as well.

Today you have been given life, and I wonder if you realize how many people are impacted by your words and deeds. The impact you have on another may be seemingly small and insignificant to some, but you never know how many lives you touch. Don't be afraid to give what you have to another today; after all, it just might be what they need.

Reflect:

When has someone journeyed with you in a time of suffering? Recall the experience. Who do you need to journey with as they suffer?

❖ ❖ ❖

Goodbye

◆ ◆ ◆

Jesus Dies on the Cross

I don't even remember when I went to Nova Scotia, Canada for the first time, but it was many years ago. I have a lot of great memories about that trip, many of which involve food and some incredible Tim Horton's goodness as well as meeting some fantastic people. The story of the trip ends, though, with me splitting my pants. I have a vague recollection of the event; but to be honest, it wasn't the first time I'd done so, and I am sure it won't be the last. I am like the hulk, except I never rip my shirt. Now that you are sufficiently uncomfortable let's continue. Apparently, I asked a deacon's wife named Jocelyn to mend them for me. Ha! She did, and then I dared to ask her to take me to a store so I could buy socks. In retrospect, I can deduce that I threw something other than appropriate clothing in a suitcase, some old shoddy pants, and no socks, thinking this was sufficient for Canada. Good grief!

Years passed, and I found myself back in good ole Halifax where the Deacon Mark and his wife tell the story of our first encounter. She sat on a comfortable chair with a breathing machine hard at work. Since I'd seen her last, she was in an all-out fight with cancer, and it had been a challenging year. We all talked and ate some fantastic food while we reminisced. She wasn't going to be able to go to the event I was at, but, as it was understood, she wasn't going to many things as of late. Her health was in a steady decline.

I returned a year later and my friend John picked me up from the airport. I asked my friend John how Deacon Mark and Jocelyn were doing. He said that she was in emergency care now and was dying. I asked if it would be okay to visit them, and so a call was made. I was invited to a very holy place that day. As I walked into the room I saw many familiar faces. Jocelyn was breathing with great difficulty and all the while her husband held her hand. We talked and laughed about socks and split pants. As I was sitting there, a priest came in to visit. He kissed her forehead. She was loved and remembered by so many. The priest said that the number of rosaries that Jocelyn made in her life was like a storehouse of graces from all of the prayers people had prayed due to her insistence at making them for people to use. The bishop was already there earlier that day and gave her blessings, and family and friends had brought cards. Why was I, an outsider, given such a spot in such a vulnerable time for them? As I was about to leave, Deacon Mark told me that it was their 39th wedding anniversary that day. He loved her still. I asked if I could take a photo of him holding her hand. It was respectful, and he agreed. She died two days later. As I left Nova Scotia, I was so grateful to have said goodbye to such a quiet saint. I am confident she is going to have something to say to me if I forget to bring my socks with me to heaven!

Death can be scary. It is unknown and marks a transition from one state of being to the next. It is hard to say goodbye to loved ones and confront the reality that one day we also are going to die. What is it about our faith that can cause a couple on their very anniversary to find joy amidst death? It is Jesus. The last sorrowful mystery focuses on Jesus' death on the cross. Imagine being around as Jesus breathes His final breath — only a handful of His closest friends remained to actually see the moment. It probably felt final. They were likely heartbroken. But death wasn't the end. In Jesus, death is never the end. There is resurrection in Christ. That is what allowed Mark and Joceyln to celebrate their 39th anniversary with joy. They knew Jesus and trusted that death wasn't the end — it was just another part of the journey.

I think I need to know Jesus more. There is something about the way that joy works that is beyond the constant instability of life, and I want that joy in an ever-increasing measure. I think it comes down to trust. Trusting that God knows and does, in fact, love, even when great loss and hurt seem to prevail, is the catalyst for joy. If God has only good things in store for us, then in our storms and trials, the brokenness, or even facing mortality, joy can be found. Joy can be found, because God is with us in our sorrow.

Reflect:
Do you know anyone who has a radical trust in Jesus, even in times of suffering? What qualities do they possess that you can grow from?

SECTION FOUR:
THE GLORIOUS MYSTERIES

◆ ◆ ◆

Resurrection of Christ

Ascension of Jesus

Descent of the Holy Spirit

Assumption of Mary

Coronation of Mary

As we approach the glorious portion of this book, it may seem obvious that our glorious moments are filled with joy. Bearing that in mind, we can also put some unrealistic expectations of needing to have big "glorious" moments in our lives to have joy. We reason: "Without the big moments, there can't be big joy."

Glorious moments happen in our daily routine; we often just miss them. To find the glorious moments is to look at the relational experiences that point us to understanding the glory of God. Each of our glorious moments, especially those we experience daily, can open our hearts to the reality of who God is. In other words, I believe that God intentionally made us in a way that our experiences help us to see and know Him. Without the willingness to look for God's glory in our relational moments, there is often going to be many things that we simply consider a highlight reel rather than a gift from God meant to invite us to see Him in our daily routine and to seek Him in all we do.

If we can find the glory of God at work in our every day moments — especially within our relationships — we will certainly have something rich to reflect upon when it comes to the way in which God loves us.

Saying Yes

◆ ◆ ◆

Resurrection of Christ

When I asked Linda to be my wife many years ago, there was only one answer that I wanted her to give. I asked, "Will you marry me?" and (in case you were wondering) she said, "Yes." I understand some cultures still have arranged marriages, but in our basic understanding of love, especially within the Catholic context, a free response is necessary in love. We can't make someone love us.

If you look at the Sacred Scriptures, the idea of a call followed by a response is a very common way of understanding various narratives. Look at many Old Testament examples of faith, and you will see a call and response. Noah is called to build an ark, and he responds with an obedient "yes." Abraham is called to offer his son as a sacrifice, to which he says "yes." Samuel the prophet hears the voice of God and responds, "Here I am Lord." Jonah calls out to the people of Ninevah to repent, and they respond by repenting. The ultimate example is, of course, Mary who hears the voice of an angel and responds, "Be it done unto me according to your word." But there are also times where people do not respond positively to the call of God. We can think of the times in the Gospels when Jesus is accused falsely or when the Pharisees are judgmental and attempt to lure Him into a verbal trap. There are even regions where Jesus is unable to do the miracles He did in other regions because of the lack of faith the people in that area demonstrate. I imagine most people reading this book would prefer to be a positive responder rather than ignore the call of God in our life.

When we think of a personal response to the call of God, too often people seem to assume that this is primarily a Protestant spiritual activity. For Catholics, we begin our journey of faith at baptism, but our response should be happening all the time. We respond to the liturgical cadence at Mass by joining in the responses. We reaffirm our baptismal promises and should be reminded of that new beginning each time we dip our finger in the holy water font and make the Sign of the Cross. We certainly are not a "one and done" type of people. There is an ongoing conversion that we are invited to personally respond to and that "yes" should continue until we enter into eternity.

I've been married to Linda for over 25 years, and it is a comfort to know that she freely chooses my company over all others. We both give our "yes" to one another daily by responding to each other's needs. We work, dream, talk, and act in a way that is a constant "yes" to one another. Was there a first yes? Of course. But to think that marriage is only about one response to an initial call is unthinkable. A growing relationship is centered upon the freedom of growth and of continually becoming and exploring new opportunities together. A loving relationship is about stretching and exploring, seeking and finding all the while with the one you have freely chosen to walk beside. Our spiritual lives are a similar opportunity to freely grow and respond to love's call.

What exactly are we responding to? Jesus' invitation to new life, and it happens through the Resurrection. Without Jesus' bodily Resurrection, little of what we do makes sense. What does it matter if we have a personal relationship with Jesus? If we believe that Jesus rose from the dead and we believe that by following Jesus we will also rise from the dead, it makes an eternal difference. The first glorious mystery calls our attention to this "resurrection event" that changes everything. Jesus died but rose again; and it is through this dying and rising that we are saved from our sins and heaven is opened to us. This is what we call "good news." And it demands a response.

Every day is an opportunity to respond deeper to the love of God, but we have to be willing to listen. We have to give our personal "yes." In many ways, as Catholics, this reminder that we have to choose our faith is reinforced on a regular basis. We can choose to go and be healed in the Sacrament of Reconciliation. We can choose to go forward and receive the Eucharist, proclaim the word "Amen," meaning, "so be it." In that moment, as we say "Amen," it is like we are saying, "Be it done unto me according to thy word." We can say "yes" to our call and respond in a manner that impacts those around us by giving drink to the thirsty, food to the hungry, and all the other corporal works of mercy. Our faith is one that is a constant personal "yes." I hope you can see how God is calling you a little deeper today, and my prayer is that you will respond to the call with a saintly "yes." This is one decision you will never regret.

Reflect:
How will you respond "yes" to Jesus daily?

◆ ◆ ◆

New Life

♦ ♦ ♦

Ascension of Jesus

When Linda and I got married at the age of 21, we realized within the first few months of our new life together that we wanted to be open to the possibility of a baby. We had dated for years, so by the time we had officially tied the knot, we couldn't think of too many reasons why holding off on having children would be to our advantage. It isn't as if we went out and immediately made it our mission to become parents, but we decided that trusting God could include our fertility. Within a few months we found out we were pregnant, and we had no idea how much our lives would change.

I can't remember how Linda shared with me that we were pregnant, but I know that our parents were not excited about us having children so early in our marriage. Linda and I were excited and filled with great anticipation until we took the Lamaze class. The instructor talked about "phases" and "dilation," which was enough to emotionally unsettle me, but it was when she started showing the videos of people having home births (one of them was her home birth) that things began to get frightening. We left that class terrified. The consolation was knowing that people had given birth to children since the dawn of humanity, so somehow, when our time came, we would figure it out.

When Linda went into labor, we found ourselves at St. Mary Hospital in Royal Palm Beach, Florida. The contractions had been difficult for some time, and we spent a long period of time walking the hallways that were unfinished from the construction they were doing on that particular wing. As the labor pains continued and the time seemed to slip by, we found that the baby's heartbeat would slow down during the contractions. There was great alarm as to why this was happening, and we were very close to having to have an emergency C-section. Linda was in labor for so long, and she was unwilling to have any medication to alleviate the pain. When our baby was finally born, we found that the umbilical cord was around her neck, explaining the decrease in the heartbeat with every contraction. She was healthy but very tiny. Six pounds and 1/4 ounce with itty bitty ears sticking out from her perfect little head. She was alive and well, adorable, and ours. Linda was exhausted, and I was an emotional wreck.

When we left the hospital the car seat was so big Hannah seemed to be this tiny baby doll instead of a real little human. We arrived at our home in West Palm Beach and began the new journey of taking care of a person that was entirely dependent upon us. Linda was unwavering in her commitment, doing all she could to help this baby be on a schedule for both of their sanity. Hannah spent a lot of time in a beautiful bassinet that we could put at the foot of our bed.

This new life taught us many things about ourselves that we previously had no way of knowing. First, I think it was clear to me that I needed to work harder to make sure I could take care of my family. Those were days of almost working non-stop to ensure we had money to pay our bills. Linda was learning that if she deviated from the schedule, our little Hannah would be fine and wouldn't grow up to be a serial killer. We became experts at changing diapers, getting her burped and settled after meals, and tried to help her enjoy the Florida sun by taking walks and going into the local pool. We were learning what it looked like to be a family. No longer were our dreams just for Linda and myself, but would forever include our little Hannah.

Those days are so long ago, and thankfully we have many photos and incredible memories of our new little family. Hannah is now married, lives in Las Vegas, and is beginning her own little family. Her new beginning as a parent will be so much different than ours. She has a husband that makes decent money, and although he travels for work, they have great opportunities for vacations and times of getting away together. I worked so much that even my weekends were packed with jobs to pay our bills. Now, we are in the age of surfing the web, learning everything about anything that is of interest by going to YouTube, and flipping through thousands of television shows that can meet almost every interest that is out there. We had no internet, no cell phones, and could barely afford "basic" television. It isn't bad; it is just the way it was back then. Linda was just saying the other day that if we would have had the internet back then like we do now, things would have been incredibly different.

The glorious reality of becoming parents and learning how to make decisions together as husband and wife that would impact the child we had together was, in so many ways, a taste of heaven. To see Linda and me in this tiny little child who was entirely her person was mind-blowing. Little Hannah was fast on her feet, learning to walk at an early age. She was extremely articulate with an adorable little voice. But not everything was easy and effortless by any means.

Because this was our first child and our parents were hours away from us, we were, in many ways, alone. Linda would spend countless hours by herself watching little Hannah while I worked. There were many things that hurt us — primarily being apart for so long — but at that time, it was our only option. I was also unsure of how to deal with Hannah when she got older or was disobedient. How do we discipline in a way that works and affirms our love? Should we homeschool or put her in public school? What we realized is being a new parent meant new beginnings — constantly. One of the things we eventually realized is that this is our family, our story, and our decision to make, whatever that may be at that moment. We had been entrusted by God with this little life, so we could move forward with a bit more confidence, even if we were so young.

Life is full of new beginnings and moments when everything changes. When Jesus was raised from the dead, He stayed with the disciples for a little while, helping them understand what happened and preparing them for their new beginning. The second glorious mystery focuses on the Ascension of Jesus. In a final moment reminiscent of a movie, Jesus is taken up into heaven, and His disciples are left looking at the sky. Angels are there, and they charge the disciples to go — the mission starts. It was a new beginning. They needed to find new courage to boldly speak, heal, cast out demons, and be persecuted for their faith. The early community had to resolve conflicts, determine what rules and guidelines they would live by, and decide how to integrate (or not) with the Jewish and Roman community. New beginnings can be overwhelming. We trust, though, that even when we cannot see Jesus His presence is still with us. We are still being guided, and we shouldn't fear. Just like God prepared Linda and I for Hannah (and the rest of our kids), God has prepared you for your new beginnings. There might be bumps in the road or big questions, but God gives you all the grace you need for that first start — He never leaves you alone.

Reflect:
Where is there a new beginning in your life? How can you invite Jesus into that beginning?

◆ ◆ ◆

Protecting What Is Ours

◆ ◆ ◆

Descent of the Holy Spirit

Many years ago, my family moved from Florida to Ohio. This was an epic task for a family such as ours. In Florida we settled into a home near both of our parents and siblings, I had some contacts for the ministry I was doing and would likely be able to keep busy, and the house we recently moved into was perfect for a growing family such as ours. We decided to leave everything and move to a place in Ohio that was very unfamiliar to us, where no family lived to help us in our time of need, and had little to no ministry contacts that could guarantee a busy season. We were convinced that Ohio was where our family was called to be, so we sold our home and rented the largest truck and trailer we could from Uhaul and left everything and everyone to start over in a land we knew not.

The wonderful neighborhood we moved into had a strong religious presence, including numerous theologians teaching at the local university and some known ministers and lay evangelists. On Friday evenings, the neighbors would gather near the religious formation house and begin a "rosary walk" that covered about a mile within our little neighborhood. The neighbors prayed for the city and our streets, asking God to work in and through one another. It was glorious! That first year we met some wonderful and faith-filled families and were invited to attend a celebration up the road at the religious order's residence. The entire neighborhood seemed to be invited. Kids played in the streets, and religious sisters wearing long flowing habits mingled with the families present all the while talking about life and faith, family and the legacy of this particular order. Food was served, drinks and desserts were offered, and the afternoon flew by with great celebration.

Later that evening we made our way down to our home feeling blessed that God had called us to such a land of rich spiritual people. When we got home, we saw that our door was open. No worries though — we lived in heaven on Earth — so what if we left the door open. But I hadn't left the door open. I am a bit neurotic about things like that, and while we may have left the door unlocked, I couldn't see leaving it wide open.

As we walked into our home, I realized someone had been inside. The first thing I observed was that my laptop was gone. As we began to search our home, we noticed our DVD player and some discs were missing. My amazing camera with all the different lens attachments was also gone. The reality of having been robbed rushed in with a sobering weight, and I felt violated. Who does that? How can someone come in and go through our property and leave with things that are not their own? The laptop was a huge blow. All my ministry contacts were in it, and knowing I had to somehow start over in collecting the information I had painstakingly gathered was overwhelming. For years afterward, as we drove through our neighborhood, I would tell my kids to keep their eyes open for a compact Presario laptop computer. We never found it.

The truth that evil can move and be found within so much goodness was one lesson that we revisited often during those years in Ohio. Neighbor's cars were broken into, drugs were sold in nearby streets, and shootings were reported not far from our street. Every day to get to my house, I would pass through a rough neighborhood. Over the years, a convent moved in two houses down from ours, another home housed priests coming for a period of rest and renewal, and the rosary walk continued with steady resolve. The neighbors would be invited to celebratory events, but doors were secured, and our monthly investment in a security system was one that we were faithful to pay. It wasn't that our area was the worst place to live in that small town; rather, it was that I had a false understanding of where I was living. I needed to look at my surroundings and assess the land to make wise decisions. I couldn't live under the delusion that we had somehow arrived at the Promised Land when, in fact, there was evil all around.

This has been a great lesson for me when it comes to my spiritual growth. There are times in our life when we think that we are in such a great place of spiritual consolation and security. We find ourselves encouraged and uplifted, maybe even feeling like we are on top of the world. What could go wrong? If we are not careful, we can let our guard down and the enemy can establish a foothold in our life. The need for spiritual readiness is something that St. Paul talks about with the armor of God. The description given is one of preparing for battle (you can read it yourself in Ephesians 6:10-18). The breastplate of righteousness, feet shod with the Gospel of peace, and the sword of the spirit all are necessary for a person going into battle. The image is not lost when it comes to Catholic teaching. We are the Church militant, and while you may not hear that imagery used when speaking about the people of God, it is a classic depiction of what the spiritual life is like for us living in time. There are an adversary and many enemies that want to steal our joy, kill our faith, and destroy all that is good. The battle with the world, flesh, and the devil is so real that the Church reminds us to fight against the momentum of our culture of death, tame and control our appetites, and fight the lies of the serpent. If we are not people willing to defend what God has given to us, then we will be robbed. Saint Paul talks about us as being more than conquerors through Christ Jesus. We have to remember that we have been set up for success when it comes to the spiritual life. If we are willing, we experience moments of heaven upon Earth in our fellowship and communion with others. But we can also know that when the enemy comes to try and take what is ours, we can not only defend and keep what God has entrusted to us, but we can be an example of due diligence to those around us.

We are given the strength for this fight through the Holy Spirit. When you were baptized and confirmed, you received the Holy Spirit in a powerful way. The third glorious mystery reflects on the descent of the Holy Spirit at Pentecost. Until this point, the disciples were afraid of the mission ahead of them. They weren't exactly sure if they could face the potential persecution and challenges that were ahead, but when they received the Holy Spirit, they had all they needed.

The enemy wants to violate us, but God has empowered us to protect what He has given. There will certainly be times when we forget to close the door, or lock and set the alarm, and it is possible there will be consequences for such negligence. But God is inviting us to be "ready" at all times as if we are an army called into battle or given the task of protecting what we have obtained. The glorious truth is that everyone is in this army of God together, and our leader extends to us the ultimate of victories.

Reflect:
What do you have in your life that is worth protecting? Is your faith one of those things? In what ways can you protect and share your faith right now?

◆ ◆ ◆

Moving Toward Peace

◆ ◆ ◆

Assumption of Mary

The older I have gotten, the more I have embraced the pursuit of peace. Many things in my life do not lead me toward this cherished peace. I have attempted to find ways to rid them from my daily experience. Linda and I spend a lot of time dreaming about what we want to do. It is a glorious part of our marriage. Often the dreams are so exciting that we seem captivated by them for months. Some of the dreams we have entertained lasted brief periods of time but were fun while they lasted. Our dream of moving to a homestead was a long, aching journey, so much so that we often wondered whether it would come to pass.

I think what we were looking for was a place to call our own where we could try new things and explore options and possibilities based on our willingness to learn. We wanted to have an oasis. We were certainly grateful for what we had and were not prone to spend our time lamenting our situation, but we did feel like God had placed a desire in our hearts to take another giant leap toward fulfilling our dream to become homesteaders.

One of the most exciting things about this new dream was the idea of being a bit removed from neighbors and drama. We had enough issues on our own without adding neighborhoods to our plate. Silence is a constant opportunity to think about how beautiful God is and how present He can be without all the distractions. We moved to central New York — our silent oasis — to fulfill a dream when we finally bought the homestead, but if truth is told, we certainly didn't wait until we left Ohio to begin that dream.

We started the pursuit of peace in our home in Ohio where I learned how much I enjoyed building things and how I loved, even more, destroying other things. We built a chicken coup and rabbit hutch, we deconstructed our deck, and we put patio stones down. We worked alongside family and friends as we cut a third of our garage off and created an English garden with a wonderful trellis. In other words, we created as many opportunities for peace as we could find. While we were blessed and grateful for what we had, we also knew that God was fanning into flame, even more, this dream to create a family legacy on a homestead.

When we began our journey, we realized that there would be a lot of work to do before we could be settled but had little idea the amount of work that would be. Our septic system was a mess, the electric was chaotic, and the well was not clean. We had problems with the land from logging trucks, and we purchased a house that wasn't insulated with winter fast approaching. We had epic taxes to pay, surveys and appraisals to address, and a very real issue of where our daughter and granddaughter would stay when they came to visit us. We looked into RV's and trailers and even renovating our garage into an apartment. We priced sheds and struggled with the reality of not having enough rooms for the rest of the family if we brought them into our home to sleep. Finally, we ended up meeting a man who had a hunter's cabin that was ready to go with a little wood burning furnace and some insulation. They moved it onto our property, and we finished it off with more insulation and a bit of elbow grease to make it a home. Our run down and once neglected home was slowly transforming into a place we could start to live our dream out a bit more than previously imagined.

The trip from the airport to my home now touches me deeply. It isn't a far-off dream anymore. We are living out our dream that was an ache and great labor of love. The constant feeling of being home and of feeling that peace is such a blessing, especially knowing that we have so much work before us. The kitchen is now my current office, and the actual office is where our bedroom is because the present kitchen is where our future bedroom must be. There are wood sheds to be built, a barn that needs to go up sooner than later, and a list a mile long of what we want to see happen. Peace is not an easy thing to find, but it is funny how glorious it is to be where you know you are called to be, and how much peace can be present amidst the hard work and sweat-stained clothes. We have a long way to go, but this journey toward peace is already more amazing than we could have imagined.

While we aren't there yet, the peace we feel comes from knowing where we want to be. We look forward at what we hope is coming in the future and that gives us strength for today. The fourth glorious mystery of the rosary is about the Assumption of Mary. When Mary's time on Earth is over, she is assumed into heaven — she is taken up body and soul. Mary was set apart for Jesus' birth, so this unique transition from life on Earth into eternity isn't unusual. So what makes it worth reflecting on? Because, one day, you and I will exist in eternity as both body and soul. That is the peace of heaven. Mary foreshadows what God wants for us and precedes us by entering into heaven, body and soul intact. Living our Christian life can be hard, especially when we seem far off from whatever perfect vision we have of discipleship. We may see a house that still has a long way to go, but God isn't finished with us. Just as Mary was taken up perfectly into heaven, body and soul, God desires the same from us. In the meantime, our role is to do what we need to do on Earth to try to be holy and focus on taking our walk of discipleship one day at a time.

Reflect:
Where are you most at peace?

◆　◆　◆

Even More Life

◆ ◆ ◆

Coronation of Mary

We have nine children. Most people know this if they've done any exploration into my life and ministry. I talk a lot about my kids and have told countless stories over the last 20 years about them. I have learned a lot about fatherhood and what it means to be a child of God because of my kids. I've learned that I needed my kids to help teach me who God is, as well.

What most people don't know is that we have had five miscarriages. We don't talk about them. When people ask how many children I have, I always say nine; five girls and four boys. If asked what their names are I recite with ease: Hannah, Sarah, Madeline, Noah, Kolbe, Mary, Jude, Joseph, and Ella. It would be too complicated to go into the five children, whom we love dearly but will never get to know fully on this side of eternity. The five miscarriages have been painful for our family, but we are thankful to have some Padgett's praying for us in heaven.

As married couples, to be open to more life within a family means to be open to the possibility of loss. The problem with this is that most people don't talk about miscarriages. In fact, many people don't know what to say when they hear of a family member who passes or a friend who is sick and in the hospital. While it is difficult to face one's mortality, we at least have an arsenal of things we can say like, "Sorry for your loss," or, "Praying you feel better." When some people hear of a miscarriage, they don't seem to know what to say. So often the parents do not even disclose this news of this loss to close friends. If the couple has had a few miscarriages over the years, it is probable no one knows about them because they wait to tell others of pregnancy after longer and longer periods of time. There are many misunderstandings from people when they hear about a miscarriage, especially if the couple that miscarried has other children. Somehow it doesn't seem as much like a loss to others because they never really saw the baby, don't know the personality, and the couple has other children, so ultimately it seems odd to mourn. But many couples mourn, because they know that baby is real. We heard the heartbeat of Felicity, and then a couple of weeks later Linda miscarried her. Linda's tenacious personality did all she could to save any remains, and we were able to bury her and had a service in which the entire family was present. Linda honored these children with a beautiful tattoo, which was an honest and heartfelt attempt at permanently memorializing these children who love us entirely. We have named them all and know that one day all of us will have the chance to see the way in which God allowed us to be a family in such a unique manner.

The beauty of life is a profound witness of God who is life. Each child is a declaration of God's generosity, even amidst a time of loss. In a time where the world has a growing disinterest in devaluing life at all stages, for families willing to be open to children, the probability of experiencing this type of loss is increasingly greater.

Whenever I find out a friend of ours has had a miscarriage, I feel a sense of sadness and loss, knowing that this family will not have the chance to see the child's beautiful personality, quirks, and mannerisms. It is a true loss, and yet the hope of their love and involvement within the family is present. This faith in a God who is life does, in fact, bring about a true hope of an eventual reunion. Some of our friends have been very quiet about their losses, and we can certainly understand. The idea of telling everyone you are pregnant and then having to later answer the countless questions about how the pregnancy is going, baby names, and milestones can be just too much for families to answer with the pain still so fresh. It seems easier just to remain quiet. I think mourning and rejoicing go hand in hand with all of life, and in some ways, inviting the faithful community to be a part of those moments is a true gift that should be cherished. The beauty of life is glorious, and I am thankful that we have had the children we have, both those with us and those cheering us on.

The final glorious mystery reflects on Mary being crowned as Queen of Heaven and Earth. The image comes from the Book of Revelation, which details an end to suffering and the ultimate triumph of Jesus Christ over evil. In this vision, all things are made new. Families are reunited, wars cease, and God reigns. It is a place where every tear is wiped from the eyes of those who mourn. When we reflect on Mary being crowned, this newness should come to mind. The glory of this mystery is that God is always drawing us toward something greater, even in great pain.

Reflect:
What do you believe heaven is like?

SECTION FIVE:
THE LUMINOUS MYSTERIES

◆ ◆ ◆

Baptism of Jesus

Wedding at Cana

Proclamation of the Kingdom of God

The Transfiguration

Institution of the Eucharist

The Luminous Mysteries present a new challenge for us; after all, how can our life story be "luminous"? What does this mean for our everyday experiences? Over the years I have realized that many moments in our life help us to learn powerful and important lessons about who we are and how we can love. These moments reveal to us not only information about ourselves but also help us in understanding the glory of God. Each of our "luminous" moments, whether it is something we experience individually or collectively with those we are in a relationship with, can open our hearts to the reality of ourselves, others, and God. In other words, I believe that God intentionally made us in a way that our experiences help us to learn about ourselves and others and aid in seeing and knowing Him. Without the willingness to look for God's insights in our relational moments, there are going to be many things that we simply consider a highlight reel rather than a gift from God meant to invite us to look "up." We all have a lot to learn and those luminous moments should be treasured. I think it is clear that each of the moments within the joyful, sorrowful, and glorious parts of our life should be ones we are learning from, and I would say that they are, but this section captures the ability to learn in even the seemingly mundane and average moments of our day. When we see our luminous moments, where love triumphs in the daily experiences, we are shown a bit more about who God is. If we can find these illumined moments of God at work, at home, and in our daily life, we will certainly have something insightful to reflect upon when we consider the way in which God loves us. What a revealing and insightful truth to consider! What an opportunity for joy as we allow Him to shine the light on our life.

◆　◆　◆

Baptism, Not Baby Dedication

◆ ◆ ◆

Baptism of Jesus

My mother kept several scrapbooks from my younger years, and I used to spend a fair amount of time going through them. The paper was brittle and old with glue finally unable to hold the pictures in place. I loved looking at the old baby pictures, and my mother was quite meticulous, even saving lockets of hair and some baby teeth. This is more than a little disconcerting to me as an adult.

One day, while going through one of these scrapbooks, I found a sheet of paper that turned out to be a baptismal record. I about went through the roof with joy. I was raised in a Protestant home where we were decidedly not Catholic. When I was younger, I can vividly recall giving my life to Christ at a Nazarene church and following this with what was called "believer's baptism." This was, as far as I knew, my only baptism to date. When I found the sheet of paper from St. Luke's Lutheran Church, I confronted my mother asking her why I had never been told I was baptized as an infant. To this, my mother responded that to her it wasn't a baptism; it was more of a "baby dedication."

The funny thing for me, as a recent convert to Catholicism, is I knew that this infant baptism was my true beginning as a follower of Christ. My mother may have wanted it to only be a dedication, but when I was baptized in the name of the Father, the Son, and the Holy Spirit, I was born again! That certificate is now framed and a constant reminder that God has had me in His hands from the very beginning. In so many ways, realizing I had been given to Jesus as a baby was like being given a few extra volumes of an epic novel that was truly my own.

Sacred Scripture is not afraid to emphasize and speak about beginnings. We see the beginning of the earthly and heavenly beings, the beginning of the human race, the beginning of the nations and first civilization, and, ultimately, we see the beginning of the Incarnation, the public ministry of Jesus, and eventually the beginning of the new Church. Each of us is invited into the beauty of new beginnings because such a glorious opportunity is a part of what it means to be Christ's followers.

Jesus' public ministry begins with His baptism in the river Jordan, and we meditate on that moment in the first luminous mystery. John baptizes Jesus, and then God the Father speaks, "This is my beloved Son, with whom I am well pleased." Those profound words were spoken to you (even if they weren't audible) at your baptism as well. They were spoken to me as an infant, even though I didn't realize it. God, that day, brought me into His family. I went into the water an orphan and came out a son of God.

While my parents may not have understood the magnitude of my baptism as a child, God took to willing hearts, albeit a bit unknowing, and accepted this little child. I have been His for a lot longer than I realized, and I couldn't be happier. Not only did baptism give me a new beginning, but it gave me a true belonging, within a family, and enabled me to do great things.

As Catholics, our baptisms are of such importance that on major feast days we will reaffirm our baptismal promises. When we enter a Church, we dip our fingers into the holy water font and make the Sign of the Cross over ourselves. This is a reminder of our baptismal promises and the fact that we are buried with Him in Baptism and raised to newness of life.

When I was finishing my RCIA experience, Linda and I decided to have our children baptized even before we had finished the course ourselves. We were so convinced that Baptism was imperative that I asked my friend Father John to baptize my three girls. We didn't know anyone who was Catholic, so he became their godfather. What was beautiful was to have that same priest baptize the child of the child he had baptized so long ago and to have that same priest witness the marriage of another of those children as the presiding priest at my daughter's wedding. Baptism brings us together, allows us to become family, and begins anew a life that has everything it needs for success.

Reflect:
Imagine God the Father speaking these words to you, "You are my beloved child." What is your reaction? Spend some time meditating on that phrase and how you respond to it.

◆ ◆ ◆

I'm Not Alone

◆ ◆ ◆

Wedding at Cana

One of the things I have been learning about myself is that I am not alone in how I feel. I can remember watching the movie "Shadowlands," which gives an account of C.S. Lewis' life. There is a line in that movie that has always stuck with me. "We read to know that we are not alone." I am an avid book lover. I can honestly say that I have no problem purchasing books, even knowing that it may be years before I get to them. I have an unquenchable appetite to learn and understand, and maybe it is because I am seeking to find others who can relate to my crazy perspectives and dreams. While that is true, I do think I am also fascinated with why people do what they do, and I can always find room for a great mystery or epic fantasy to take me away to a place where I don't have to think deep thoughts.

Something is consoling about sharing a concern or feeling and finding out that many others completely agree. In many ways, there will always be those people who will complain no matter how hard you try and please them; but they are usually pretty unhappy people, and I am learning not to give them too much of my attention and time.

I recently gave a talk to some youth leaders in the New York area. I was very honest about many of the struggles and frustrations I had gone through this year and wanted to speak with them as equals rather than placing myself in a position that would imply I was better than them. It was an amazing time, and it was powerful to hear a few of those gathered share about what God had been speaking to them about. I remember my first talk was on the idea that you can't give what you don't have. This may sound familiar to you! The call to place our brokenness in the loving heart of Jesus was presented in my talk, and then the participants walked upstairs and spent about 20 minutes in adoration and prayer. As they came back and reflected on what God spoke to them about, I realized that each of these leaders also struggled with feeling inadequate and insecure. It is amazing how similar we all are when you decide to take away the masks and break down the walls. We are not alone, and if truth be told, we are all so very similar. I am not clear as to why we have held to a notion that spiritual maturity means we are in a position for everyone to look up to us as modern day gurus. I am more and more thankful that my ministry is based on my willingness to be as real as possible. This vulnerable tactic keeps me from becoming a pain in everyone's backside.

This universal truth that each of us is broken and in need of healing is something that I know our Church tries to get into our hearts with each Mass. We publicly proclaim that we are people who have greatly sinned, and as a body, we cry out for the Lamb of God to have mercy upon each one of us. The universality of our wounded hearts is the foundation from which we reach out with hope to a God that reveals Himself as love. We all have the same story. I think this truth is why the song "Amazing Grace" has an almost unprecedented appeal. "Amazing grace that saved a wretch like me..." That lyric isn't memorized and sung with a passion because we all think it is great poetry; rather, it is sung with confidence because we are all that wretch the song is highlighting. This common need for mercy is one that will never go away, and I find it unsettling that so many prefer a person who is more experienced at pretending to be better than others than one who is willing to be seen as fully human.

Unfortunately, we hide the parts of our lives that are "wretched" from Christ and, because of that, we can never have those parts saved. Jesus attends a wedding feast in Cana, and after the third day the wine runs out. All that is left are washing basins filled with dirty water (because they are, after all, washing basins). Jesus turns that water into wine — really good wine — and uses it for something good (celebrating the wedding). If the waiters refused to pull from that dirty water and refused to listen to Christ, the miracle doesn't take place. If we refuse to acknowledge the places of our lives that are in need of healing, then we sit with stagnant water.

I don't believe we will be rewarded in heaven for having convinced everyone that we have it all together and are perfect before we enter eternity. I am confident that the truthful gaze of our Lord will be able to look past all our facades and bring our authentically broken self into the foreground to be acknowledged once and for all as who we are. It isn't a vindictive stripping of falseness, nor is it a hateful and spiteful attempt at giving the human person what he is due. I believe the Lord invites us to be honest about our weak and broken hearts and our propensity to sin in all its selfish expressions because Jesus is ready to begin a work of healing that will enable our earthly experience to be far more abundant. Heaven will not applaud our plastic presentations and false selves, but I have a feeling that when we are stripped to our utter helpless and naked reality that this moment will be one of deep recognition and healing. Why? Because it is there that we can begin to look around at others in their brokenness and have true sympathy for someone other than ourselves.

I believe as we are utterly aware of our flaws and deep propensity to hide behind our masks and walls, that entire nakedness before the Lord will be the freedom that we have longed for but have been so afraid to pursue. The peace in realizing that everyone else is in that same position can allow us to invite, with confidence, God's love to flow in and through us without restriction.

While we won't be rewarded in heaven for our ability to convince our community that we have arrived, I do think we will be acknowledged for the times we decided to love others in spite of facing the sobering truth of our frailty. Would you rather confide in someone who has always seemed to have his or her act together or the person who is battle worn and covered in scars from battles unspoken but seems to have found the rhythm of moving forward even if it is with a limp? I guess I am saying that I find more consolation in those with the limp because that is exactly where I am at in my life.

There is something beautiful in knowing we are not alone in our struggle, and, in the end, we will have nothing left to stand upon but our true self. That complete nakedness does not have to be something we fear if we can allow the Lord to strip us of the pride and false selves that we so eagerly adorn ourselves with. The more we can let go of the game and be the one receiving the healing from our Savior, the more we can become a gift to those around us. In the end, be at peace, for you are not alone!

Reflect:

What is one aspect of yourself that you feel you need to hide in order to be accepted? Contemplate that God knows that aspect and loves you.

◆ ◆ ◆

Snow

◆ ◆ ◆

Proclamation of the Kingdom of God

I must admit that I get a little excited when I see snow. There is something so calming about snow falling, covering the ground and wrapping the trees in a blanket of natural purity. Just the visual impact of snow covering woods, blanketing the Earth, and settling onto cars and buildings makes me so happy. I realize some of you are worried about me after this confession. I certainly can understand the desire for winter to be over and, like many of you, am not a fan of scraping my car windshield and having to wait forever for the heat to make the vehicle somewhat comfortable to drive. All that is true, and yet, snow falling speaks to me in a language conveying peace and tranquility. Tomorrow we may need to shovel a bit, or even plow so we can get kids to doctors appointments and children off to school, but for now, in this evening of reflection and contemplation, I am consoled by nature and the gift of a snow-covered ground.

When I was a child, we lived in North Dakota for some time. The snow was a near consistent presence, and I have vivid memories of icicles hanging from office buildings long enough to come up to our waist if measured. The smell of car exhaust in the frigid winter months, cheeks hot with cold, and the sensational feeling of walking into a warm home after hours of sledding were constant in those early years. I can remember my mother inviting us to take our cereal bowls outside and filing them with snow to make snow ice cream, which was simply the snow with some chocolate syrup drizzled on the top. We were poor, but I must admit that I was a fan of that type of spontaneous dessert.

There was a full body snowsuit that I had as a child that was perfect for all things snow related. We would often get so much snow that we could build amazing snow forts to hang out in while pretending that we were Eskimos. There was a rather large hill by the outdoor ice skating rink that was the most epic place to test your nerve while sledding. I was never able to go most of the way up to the top because I was terrified of flying down the hill so fast, but the memories I have are pleasant even at the less than terrifying levels. Occasionally my mother would come with us and even join in a sled ride or two, but I am not sure all that can explain why I have such an affection for snowfall as an adult.

There is something about the way that nature speaks of God's beauty that is very particular with regard to snow. I find beauty in the maple trees in full bloom, the trickle of a stream in the summer, and the lazy way frogs gather about the pond in the heat of the day. I love the tree in the summer, and I love the tree caked with snow in the winter. I think it is the many ways in which the same thing expresses beauty that gives me hope.

It is no wonder that Jesus so often used farm and nature language to describe spiritual realities. Nature speaks profoundly about God. As Jesus proclaimed the Kingdom of God, He often talked about seeds, seasons, and signs of the times. He drew on the natural beauty God had given people and helped them see a deeper spiritual meaning underneath it. He used the world around Him to help proclaim the Good News. I worry that sometimes we aren't as reflective as we could be and the message of Christ gets drowned out in our world. When I see the changing of the seasons, God speaks something profound to me.

In many ways my life is like a tree moving through the seasons. I am growing and often branching off in a variety of ways, blooming and filling my space with hopeful goodness, and yet I am also the person, in seasons of change, who is dying in many ways and holding on in the cold spiritual season I find myself within. I feel hope at spring, starting over and new life, and know that just as the tree has spent time slowing down and reflecting beauty during the winter, it will soon burst into buds that will unfold life in a green and wonderful way. The blanket of snow speaks of rest and renewal, and maybe for me that is the reminder of what will one day be true for all of us. Finding the beauty of God's love, even in our cold and desolate times, is a very important part of spiritual growth.

Being a student of the seasons is important when it comes to spiritual maturity. Knowing that just as the seasons have their rhythm and cadence, so too will those wanting to grow in their faith. We can not possibly maintain a constant spring time when it comes to spiritual growth, nor will everything remain cold and dead. I think in many ways I am learning how to be at peace with myself when I am going through the spiritual winter, rather than panicking because I somehow seem less passionate about things than I had been previously. The seasons of our spirituality are dictated by the way in which God made us and the environment in which we are growing. Allowing God to work within us in such a way is necessary, but you can find comfort in knowing that you are not somehow less grounded when it seems things are dying; it may, in fact, just be a time of autumn within your spiritual life.

Winter, especially after some time, brings with it the expectation of spring. I think sometimes watching the snow fall makes me see hope amidst the winter dying. I know that God is working in my life when I feel cold spiritually, but often I have a hard time seeing that beauty since I have very little warm fuzzy feelings validating this growing process. The blankets of snow are visual reminders to me that His beauty covers the muddy roads and barren branches, and His mercy and grace pour over me in my times of spiritual cold. Soon the snow will melt and the days will be longer, followed by the thaw, rain, and bursting buds with leaves filling the trees and flowers unfolding in gardens. Life has a cadence that can bring a sense of peace to each of us along the way. No one season is better than the other; in fact, each has a very important purpose. For me, I think I have been in a winter period for about a year. I have found a lot of beauty in dying, and although many would prefer spring and summer, I know that those seasons will be upon me before I know it. Have I learned what God wanted me to know from this season? I am not the quickest of learners, so I have a feeling some of these lessons I'll be getting again and for that I am thankful. God's love for me is often seen in a steady snowfall, a refreshing rain, and a beautiful and scenic trail. God's love is not hindered by seasons; rather, He works in me to enable me to become fertile soil. We are truly a blessed people to have a God who is the master gardener, knowing exactly what to do so that we can be cared for in cold periods so we blossom into greatness in springtime. The next time you look outside at snow, remember to look past the frozen water to see the artistic expression of a God that can show such beauty in the wintertime. Just like the seaons proclaim these truths, so our lives can proclaim the Kingdom and goodness of God. We can be reflections of the Gospel message and proclaim it, fearlessly, to the world around us.

Reflect:
How does your life reflect who God is in whatever season of life you are in now?

◆ ◆ ◆

Not Knowing

◆ ◆ ◆

The Transfiguration

I had a breakthrough moment the other day. I have faced many challenges on our little homestead. I am not upset that things go wrong, or that nature does what she will do with blizzards and thunderstorms. What makes me upset is when I do not know how to address the problem that is looming before me. It is "not knowing" that makes me want to go crazy at times.

We bought a new snow blower for the homestead, and I eagerly awaited the opportunity to use it. I bought it as a package deal and figured it was what we needed for the promised abundance of snow we would be forced to endure. Of course, the winter after we bought it we barely received any snowfall at all. We took credit for the lack of snow, because we are certain God knew that we were not ready for such happenings. Finally, one afternoon we got the snow I was hoping for. We started up the snow blower and, only because we took a video of its use that first time, realized that half of it was working and the other half was not rotating at all. Everyone I told about it said there was something wrong with the "sheer pin." My first question: What's a sheer pin? My second question: How do I fix one and where does one get said pin? Now, most people would go to this amazing new invention called the "internet," and if they simply typed "fix sheer pin on snow blower" into the search bar, they will find countless videos and information that would enable the most incapable individual to succeed where they never imagined they could. The problem with this handy tool is that we couldn't seem to get it where we lived.

So, unfortunately, I was stuck with an amazing amount of frustration, because I know that I can't even begin to consider a variety of options to makeshift a temporary fix because mechanics is not where my brain energy goes. I have a large mental backlog of information geared to write songs, tell stories, and encourage people with comedy and physical humor. If the microphone goes out at an event, I can project my voice and keep the audience's attention. If my guitar string breaks, I can play the song without drawing undue attention to the guitar. But, with mechanical issues, electric and septic problems, or even basic agricultural and farming obstacles, I am trying to find a reference point that is not even there. It is the not knowing that drives me crazy.

What I need to realize and give myself a little break over is the fact that everyone, at least starting an entirely new way of living, must begin from scratch. I can't rely on a heritage of farmers in my family because that heritage was academics, teaching, and artistic and creative expressions. This whole homesteading fix-it-on-the-fly thing is all new. I must say that I love being here nonetheless, and whatever obstacles I face I know that I am learning. That is my consolation. While it is all new for Linda and me, when our kids are older they will have a heritage and legacy of life that will allow for them to not only utilize their creativity in areas like literature, music, and photography but they will also know how to raise animals on a farm, keep a house warm with a wood burning stove, plant and harvest food, and hunt and fish and trap. And they will know how to fix a sheer pin! They will know because they learned alongside their parents.

One day we will look back and roll our eyes and shake our heads at how clueless and innocent we were, but

I think it will be with a lot of fondness. I think in some ways this is what it is like for us when we begin to live the faith on our own. Many of us have a heritage of a family going to Mass and praying daily, but a lot of you have only begun this journey of growing in your faith recently with no past reference points to help guide you. For me, I grew up in a Christian home, but both Linda and I became Catholic later in life. What was new for us in growing as "baby Catholics" is now an old hat over 17 years later. What was difficult for Linda and I to explain to our family members when we decided to become Catholic will be just who they are as they move from their youth into adulthood.

In many ways when I look at this story of going from Protestantism to Catholicism, it makes me realize that a leap from city living to off the grid homesteading isn't the most radical thing we have done. We have always been willing to follow our hearts, and I just have to remind myself that the new and unexpected moments that reveal my not knowing are simply opportunities to grow and learn more about myself and this life we have chosen. I wonder if you are struggling with something that is just a bit beyond your understanding. Maybe you've been trying to figure out why a certain thing keeps happening or you feel a certain way whenever you are around someone. Maybe you are frustrated because you just don't know how to deal with a circumstance you find yourself within. Be encouraged. You will learn a lot about yourself in this time, and while some of those moments may seem too difficult, the reality is that you will learn and grow over time — of that we can be certain.

Jesus takes a few of His disciples up a mountain to pray, but something new happens while they are there. Jesus is "transfigured" before them — His appearance literally changes — and God speaks. On top of that, Jesus is suddenly joined by Moses and Elijah, and they nonchalantly have a conversation. The disciples fall down in fear and the voice of God speaks, "This is my son, listen to Him." The disciples are about to embark on a radical journey where they won't know everything — but the key is in this simple phrase, "Listen to Him." If we can focus our lives on the voice of Christ, we can face the new challenges and uncertainties that come our way.

It is this unfolding of a moment over time that gives so much insight into why we become the persons we do. These difficulties are almost luminous and revealing, and the good news is, if we don't like what we see or how we behave in a situation, we can always change and modify until we find ourselves in a place of peace.

Reflect:
Where do you need to grow in your knowledge and understanding of your faith?

◆ ◆ ◆

Always Needy

◆ ◆ ◆

Institution of the Eucharist

I think I was under the delusion that one day I would be above the struggles with sin that accompanied me during my younger years. While there have been seasons where some sins seem more dominant than others, or a period goes by where I am not tempted in a way that used to be quite strong, I have found that sin seems to follow me throughout my good and bad days. I can say with my head that I understand we will wrestle with the world, the flesh, and the devil until we are six feet under, but for some reason I am shocked that the struggle is so real. What I am finding out is that I am not "fixed" nor do I seem to be able to really claim victory.

I remember, when I was younger, I tried to prove to God how serious I was about moving away from selfish behavior. I fostered a deep self-loathing to subject myself to a weight of punishment nowhere near worthy of my sin. I thought enough mental reprimands to prove to God once and for all that I was completely aware of how I'd failed. The last thing I wanted was to pretend that my sin was somehow allowable, acceptable, or understandable. After all, I had been bought by the blood of Jesus and no longer was under the rule of the enemy. I no longer had to give in to base urges and desires because I was filled with the Spirit, and the world and its message and trinkets would realistically become of no significance to me, if only I could just try a little harder to be committed.

One day during some early college years, I was truly overwhelmed by my past and attempted to prove my changed life by serious Scripture reading, regular prayer, and a willingness to go and speak about Christ to anyone at any time. I would take any fear I found within myself and intentionally place myself into a scenario that would take me so out of my comfort zone, just to prove to Jesus that I would not be swayed in sharing the Good News. I was miserable so much of the time, because when it came time for me to assess where I was at with simple struggles and sins, I realized I was still that messy kid who had a litany of failings a mile long. "I must be more determined," I thought, but in so many ways I was unbearable to be around both to myself and to those who were near me.

One evening I was playing some basketball, and I had such anxiety over all of my struggles, both the past and current sins I was regularly entertaining, that I felt unable to even shoot some hoops to relieve stress. I studied so much about God, read tons of books, and found that I was unable to measure up to the holiness of a God who knew all. I was aware of the severity of God's wrath toward sin and knew I had no legs to stand on. As a Protestant, so much of what was taught to me was the necessity of believing in God, regardless of one's feelings. I still think this is true, but much of my faith back then was a mental war zone. I would constantly fight the insane thoughts in my mind that were always wrestling for ground. Let's say I had a lustful thought or anger toward someone who had offended me; just having the thought would somehow prove to me that I had been somehow less than diligent in keeping my mind guarded — even if I did nothing to provoke the thought and I dismissed it immediately. I would repent of said thought, trying to prove to God that I saw it was wrong by reprimanding myself mercilessly. I figured if I showed God, by my mental flogging, that I would not tolerate any evil thought that somehow I would garner some sympathy from such a holy God. It was a habit I was becoming used to, and the scenario of acknowledging my sin would lead to a longer period of self-loathing and mental discipline. I remember that evening by the basketball courts so well, because I couldn't rid myself of my past and was unable to feel any peace no matter how often I prayed, or how much Scripture I read, or even how long and stern my verbal torture continued. In complete desperation, I cried out to God, "Lord I can't convince you to love me. Nothing I can do can make you want to be with me. If you don't want me, then I am utterly lost!" The realization that there was nothing I could do to convince God to love me was terrifying. I was living my entire life as an epic legalist, hoping to somehow be in the inner circle of God, but I just couldn't imagine Him wanting someone like me on His team.

That period was a horror, and yet the beginning of something very insightful. The God that I had subjected myself to was not the one revealed by Jesus in the Gospels. My relationship was so warped. Yet even within that place of chaos and self-loathing, Jesus was present, teaching me many things that would begin to resonate with me eventually. Sometimes we can ask why things take so long to come to spiritual fruition, and honestly, I am not sure I know the answer. What I think I need is often only what I want, and the times I try and get everything that is on my must-have list are usually the times that I am not terribly at peace, even when I have obtained the items I so tenaciously pursued.

The Lord has brought people into my life who have helped me combat this wrong thinking. One person was a guy named Bob, who showed me by his joy and friendship that the Lord loved me, regardless of my sins. I don't know why it took me so long to start to believe something I'd been taught in church my whole life, but those words of Jesus' affection began to minister to a battered and self-abused soul. The other person was my wife, Linda. In our relationship from high school, to college, and on to marriage and family, I have only had a constant picture of love and acceptance, even when my messiness is evident. Why does she love me? Why does Bob love me? Why does Jesus love me?

For some time now, I have felt that my entire life is to answer that final question. I begin to see that God's love is so steadfast and entire — that it is the catalyst inviting me into an eternity of seeing what unending love is like. In some ways, we have eternity to experience His love because time and space are too small to fully disclose its infinitude.

I will always need Jesus, and some days I feel the truth of His mercy that this is exactly the reality of my life from here on out. I will always need Jesus, and He is never inconvenienced nor irritated by this fact. I have been resting in the amazing reality that Jesus will never look at me and shake His head in disapproval that I've fallen into sin again. Having spent most of my life trying to discipline myself for every failing, it is an extremely difficult habit to break. This habitual self-loathing can oftentimes be easier to live out because it is all I've been used to for so long. I'm often afraid to believe that He, in fact, does find joy in my presence and is not irritated that I am not better than I am right now. I will always need Jesus, and He has allowed for that need to be the telling truth of His constant and ever-present love for me.

Just so you know, I certainly am not perfect in living this out. What I think it is supposed to be like is probably something like this: When I have an impure thought, say a harsh and vindictive word, entertain jealousy, envy, gluttony, or any other sin, my first thought should certainly be to say, "Lord, I am sorry..." But in practically the same breath I need to say, "...but thank you, Jesus, for never wavering in your love for me. Thank you for already forgiving this sin on the cross of Calvary. Thank you, Jesus, for the opportunity to avail me of your graces in Reconciliation, and thank you for not holding anything back concerning your love."

This love is expressed most profoundly in the Eucharist. The last luminous mystery calls us to reflect on the institution of the Eucharist at the Last Supper. It is Jesus saying, "I know you don't have it all together. I know you sometimes are incapable, it seems, of doing the right thing. But I love you so much that I am giving you my body and blood — and you get to have it as long as you are on this Earth. This is going to be my way of telling you how much I love you and how much you mean to me." It isn't a symbol that we receive; it is a person — the person of Jesus Christ.

What I have been realizing is that it always comes back to a person, who chose to love me even when I was lost in sin. He is unlike me in His commitment and love, and I am thankful to be able to learn more about what is so unnatural to me. I continue to find out more about who I am by seeing who He is, and this insight is one that I am hoping to grow in for all eternity. The need that I have is only satisfied in my Savior, and for some wonderful reason, He seems to be captivated by me.

Reflect:
What does the Eucharist mean to you? Would you live your life any differently if you could no longer receive it?

SECTION SIX:
TOWARD ETERNITY

◆ ◆ ◆

Epilogue

I felt so uncomfortable and I couldn't get into a position that would ease my discomfort. I arrived in southern Louisiana late Thursday and settled in for an upcoming conference. My bags were packed full, guitar in hand, and I knew the next few days would be busy. I found myself feeling worse as Friday arrived. Meetings, along with friends, old and new, helped offer some distraction to my increased aches and pains, but by Friday evening I was very worried that I'd somehow gotten a cold from a family member who recently visited. I sent a message asking if the symptoms included difficulty sleeping and extreme aches and pains, but nothing I had seemed to resonate with my family's colds. Saturday was so difficult that I told a team member I was going to go lie down and ended up missing something I was supposed to do during the afternoon. By evening I still couldn't get into a position that relieved my aches, and I couldn't walk ten feet without needing to pause and catch my breath. Things were not good. But being sick during the summer work season was not an option.

I was so worried on Sunday morning that I found the conference nursing staff and had them give me a quick once over. By this time, the team I was working with was aware I wasn't doing well, and I was even encouraged to sit back and let someone else jump in with my final presentations that Sunday morning. I assured everyone I was more than able to get up and finish the job I begun. The doctor and nurses looking at me were very concerned, although my blood pressure wasn't severe. They did say I was only breathing with half of my lungs and, in light of my heart history, suggested I go to a hospital down south. I assured them this would not happen. I would go home, and if I needed a doctor at least I would be by my family. By the end of Sunday afternoon, I couldn't even lift or roll my suitcase. I had to have a friend named Kris help me when we finally arrived at the airport. I was pretending all was OK, even though I was in full-fledged panic mode. I remember texting my wife saying I wasn't feeling well and thought maybe I should go to the hospital. Somehow, thanks be to God, my wife read between the lines. My connection in Charlotte felt like a two-mile sprint with an insanely tight connection. I was so exhausted and physically spent that I barely made it on the plane. I was the last to load, but because of my frequent flier status I was upgraded on the flight and didn't need to make the agonizing walk to the back of the plane. I sat in the darkened cabin's seat, trying to discern if I was going to survive this flight or not.

Everyone on the plane knew there was something wrong with me, and the flight attendant went out of her way to try and be of service. Next to me was an older lady who was traveling to visit family. Her daughter was a new flight attendant, and she was flying in first class like a queen. Looking over at me, in the middle of this flight, she asked if she could pray for me. I was so broken, unable to breathe, physically beyond uncomfortable, and I can remember thinking, "Please, yes. Please pray for me." I told her "yes." In that moment, in the darkened first class cabin, this old lady began to loudly pray in tongues over me. I was, for a split second, almost terrified, and then I realized I didn't care. I was so desperate for prayer and help that I didn't care if anyone heard. I needed help in any and every language a person could utter.

I disembarked in Syracuse, shuffling to baggage claim, wondering how I was going to pull the bags to the car where my wife waited. I will never forget coming to the car in a daze, seeing my wife, and saying that maybe I should just go home and try and sleep off this funk I was in. I am not sure why I thought sleep would help me at all, since the last few days I was in so much discomfort that sleep eluded me. Linda took one look at me and said we were going to the hospital. She had gotten one of our older kids up to watch the others, and, at midnight, my wife took my life into her hands and led us to the emergency room. The doctor later told me: "Your wife saved your life."

My aortic valve had blown. There was so much blood in my lungs that the x-ray looked like I had some growths and unknown foreign agents in my body. They secluded me off from everyone, wondering if I had an infectious disease. The people from the infectious disease department became involved and hundreds of tests were run. I was in congestive heart failure, being pumped full of medicines that would deal with possible pneumonia and any other bronchial issue. The valve was destroyed, and yet, I remember saying to the doctor that I had events that weekend but could come right back. In other words, could we just get me duck-taped up so I could do a few things and then come in for whatever quick fix was needed? The doctor looked at me and said exactly this: "You're not going anywhere."

I was devastated. Really, I had a week of ministry events coming up that would give me enough money to pay for a couple months of bills. It was all going to be gone. I felt guilty and embarrassed that I had to somehow call people to let them know I couldn't come, even though I was literally dying. I knew they would be inconvenienced. I was embarrassed thinking that I'd already had open heart surgery once — please, God, not again. Couldn't this be something else? I was afraid that people wouldn't understand, and yet in some weird way, I couldn't care about anything because I felt horrible. I remember still holding on to the possibility that I wouldn't have to have open heart surgery.

The last time I had this surgery, there were a few things that happened that really messed me up emotionally. Waking up after the surgery, you are in a "half alert, half sleep state" that is comparable to a horror movie. You are tied down, or it feels that way, and there is a tube the size of a bat shoved down your throat. You can't speak, and, in that moment, it feels as though you are dying of thirst. I ached for a drop of water on my lips. But, because of the tube in my throat, they didn't give me any water so I wouldn't throw it up. Did I mention the tube the size of a child's arm was shoved down my throat? The horror of that experience haunted me for over a decade. Sitting in the hospital, I was praying for anything but open heart surgery, because I couldn't imagine having to go through that hell again.

When the doctor came in and told me that I had to have open heart surgery, I was alone. I can't explain this moment any other way except that I sobbed. I was wrecked emotionally. My worst fear was about to happen again, and I couldn't get a handle on my emotions. I think it was soon after that my wife came in, and I told her the prognosis was not good. I thought back to the first surgery and could not believe it was happening again. Didn't I get a few more years out of this stupid pig valve? Wasn't it supposed to last a little longer? I have kids, bills, and people depending on me. I had events coming up that were not necessarily repeatable; it wasn't like I could just call and reschedule. These were events happening in a few days, and now I for sure had no hopes of going to them — that translated to lost income for my family. When you take on the role of "itinerant minister," it means that you trust that God will bring you what you need and these events were my main way of providing.

My priest came in the room and asked if I would like to go to confession, and I knew why — this surgery might be the last thing I do on Earth. I sobbed. I was an emotional basket case. We had close friends visiting, and they walked into the room, if I am recalling this correctly, and I couldn't control my emotions. I am pretty sure they are still in counseling, having dealt with seeing me in that condition.

It was around this time that my good friend Bob swept in to the rescue. He created a GoFundMe campaign and spread the word of my surgery and need for income to make up for the events I needed to miss. I don't know how he did it, but in a couple of days enough money was raised so that I could have surgery, recover, and pay bills without any worry. Mark at Franciscan University sent out a notice to staff and team members about what was happening with me and assured me that I would be prayed for and taken care of. The community of Franciscan University, especially the effort of Bob, were truly miracles for my family. I went in for open heart surgery, knowing that I was OK spiritually and that my family would be OK financially for the next few weeks while I recovered. In case you were wondering, I didn't die in that surgery either (though if I had it would give a whole new meaning to the term "ghost writer").

Now, as I write this account, several months have passed since that emergency. I still feel the aches of having one's chest cracked open, but my mechanical valve is clicking away. I am thankful and back to better health than I have experienced in years. My wife and family have poured themselves into one another and our new non-profit ministry "Catholic Family and Marriage, Inc." We realized that everything we do, from youth events to parish missions, is for the family and the betterment of marriages everywhere. Linda and I realized we were given another chance to love one another more and decided that this love was worthy of being shared. Now, more than ever, I am united with my wife and kids in helping others see the beauty of faith growing in one's family and marriage. We laugh a lot and are thankful with an acute realization that this time we have is a gift.

Joy was found in our most difficult moments, our worries and fears, and in our healing. Joy was present. How so? Joy at seeing my priest comfort my wife and my soul. Joy in seeing the team and people I'd loved and worked with offer Masses, prayers, and financial aid to my recovery. Joy was experienced when a stranger offered to pray for me on a plane from Charlotte to Syracuse. Joy was found in the crucifix that was in my recovery room, the Eucharist that was brought to me in the hospital, and the chance I had to offer up all my pain for others. Joy was found in sobbing desperately and being loved as I was. Joy was found in my children who came to visit me in the hospital. Even now, months later, I hear strangers express their joy at seeing me arrive at their parish or ministry event, knowing I had been through so much. How do I know that they knew? They tell me. "Chris, we heard about your surgery and were praying for you." I am humbled at the way the Body of Christ works and how we care for one another. I have tried to use my "platform" to bring joy wherever I go because I believe that joy is found in the person who knows that they are loved, and if there is one thing God has been trying to show me for years, it is that I am loved. You, my friends, are also entirely loved by God. So, look for the joy that is all around you and know that God has not forgotten you at all. He is still working in you even now, and if you are reading this, then you are not dead yet either!

Reflect:
What is one step you can take today to live your life and faith in a more abundant way?

LIFE TEEN
Leading Teens Closer to Christ
www.LifeTeen.com